A World Growing Old

A World Growing Old

Jeremy Seabrook

LONDON • STERLING, VIRGINIA

First published 2003 by Pluto Press
345 Archway Road, London N6 5AA
and 22883 Quicksilver Drive,
Sterling, VA 20166–2012, USA

www.plutobooks.com

British Library Cataloguing in Publication Data
A catalogue record for this book is available from the British Library

ISBN 0 7453 1840 1 hardback
ISBN 0 7453 1839 8 paperback

Library of Congress Cataloging in Publication Data

10 9 8 7 6 5 4 3 2 1

Designed and produced for Pluto Press by
Chase Publishing Services, Fortescue, Sidmouth, EX10 9QG, England
Typeset from disk by Stanford DTP Services, Northampton, England
Printed and bound in the European Union by
Antony Rowe Ltd, Chippenham and Eastbourne, England

Acknowledgements

I am deeply grateful to the Authors' Foundation (Society of Authors) for a grant which enabled me to finish this book.

I am much indebted to HelpAge International, especially to Sarah Graham-Brown, for help with contacts in India, Bangladesh and Tanzania. Their country-based reports and results of participatory research projects are always illuminating, and have supplied many of the statistics quoted in this book.

I should like to thank Mr Mongia, Dr Soneja Shubha and the staff at HelpAge India, Mr Abdul Jetha and his staff at HelpAge Tanzania and the staff of HelpAge Bangladesh. I acknowledge my debt to Madhu and Bharat Dogra in New Delhi.

I have been inspired by Simone de Beauvoir's book, *Old Age*, published in 1970. I also found stimulus in the work of Dr Gail Wilson of the London School of Economics and of Paul Johnson, Lecturer in Social History, also at the London School of Economics.

I am grateful, too, to Catherine Griffiths, Julia Cream and Tarun Pamneja of the Alzheimer's Society.

Thanks also to Age Concern in the London Borough of Brent, and especially to Charlotte Clements; to Tony Atcherley, Ted McFadyean, Percival Mars in Brighton.

I am grateful to all who have contributed to this book, including many friends with whom I am grateful to have grown older. Thanks also to Michael Edwards in Bangkok.

Some sections of this book have appeared in *The Statesman*, Calcutta, *Third World Resurgence*, *Third World Network* in Malaysia, in the *New Statesman* and *New Internationalist*. Many thanks for permission to reprint here.

Jeremy Seabrook
London
May 2003

Introduction

RESPONSES TO AGEING

The world has, over time, produced a vast range of responses towards old age. These often contradict one another, as well they might, given the ambiguities surrounding old age itself. Growing old may be regarded as a time of ripeness and fulfilment or a period of declining health and failing powers. The storehouse of human societies has amassed a great variety of ways and means of coming to terms with an experience which remains essentially *that of other people*, until, at last, it catches up with us too.

There are good reasons not to anticipate the decline that comes with ageing, not least the tendency to avoid meeting trouble halfway. Received ideas about ageing are often a means of evasion and denial. 'I'll worry about that when the time comes.' 'I'm not going to live that long.' 'I believe in living in the present.' Our own old age is almost inconceivable until it is upon us. That it is a time of serenity, or that it holds all the terrors associated with standing on the edge of eternity, are beliefs of convenience, a mechanism to distance our younger selves from our own fate.

Throughout most of recorded time old bones were rare, and the great majority of people would have died by the time they reached what we would now consider middle age. In Britain, in 1901 8 per cent of the population were over 60. By 1941 this had risen to 14 per cent. In 1991 it was 20 per cent. Today, although the old are present in increasing numbers, they nevertheless suffer a different kind of invisibility. They have become part of the landscape, obstacles on the sidewalk, impediments to the accelerating tempo of life, delaying the swiftly moving crowds in their urgent forward movement. Although they constitute one-fifth of the population, as one elderly woman in North London said, 'People look through you. If you are old and a woman, you are doubly invisible. We have become like ghosts before we die.'

The present moment inflects the ancient puzzle of old age and its meaning in ways that are historically unprecedented. In

Britain, in 2002 it was remarked that for the first time there are more people over 60 than under 16. This ought, in a democracy, to give greater power to the elderly.

Yet the testimony of the old suggests something different. Paradoxically, as they become more numerous, they observe a growing indifference towards them. It seems to them that the rich reservoir of their accumulated experience is a wasting – and often wasted – resource. They find themselves speaking an alien language to those who have little wish to understand. They no longer recognise the world they live in. 'We have lived too long' is a recurring theme.

It is remarkable that, now that the elderly are so numerous in the world, they should lament their loss of influence and power. Although in the past there were cultures which exiled or even killed their old, for the most part, when they were comparatively few, they commanded both respect and obedience. It is, perhaps, easier to create myths of wisdom and discernment in hoary heads when these are uncommon; and the nodding of senescence might well frequently have passed for sagacity.

But when life expectancy rises well into the 70s – and in Japan now, for women it is over 80 – the scarcity value of the old is undermined. The growing numbers of elderly in the world, far from representing a precious store of wisdom, are often perceived as a constraint upon the freedom and development of the young. It is not that large numbers of older people are abandoned or institutionalised. The myth of a more caring past persists, even though it has been rare for elderly parents to live with their families. In 1929–30, for instance, less than one-fifth of over-60s lived in extended families, and only 7 per cent lived in three-generation households. It was more common for people to live closer to their elderly parents than is now the case: in the dense mesh of the streets of industrial Britain, relatives often lived a few doors, or a couple of streets, away. The distance between people, which some observe today, is only partly spatial. It also psychological, since the destinies of individuals diverge more obviously than they did when most people worked in the staple industry of a single town and expected their children to do likewise.

Conflict between the generations is no new thing. All cultures tell of a new generation, eager to play its part in the life of society, excluded and often humiliated by those in positions of power and influence. And that means the old, seniors, chiefs and headmen. Youthful energy, repressed by elders, is a persistent theme.

In many societies, the authority and prestige of elders were often unlimited. In Thailand, traditional law stated that wives and children were liable for the commission of crimes by the (senior, male) head of the family. 'The liability was not due to the fact that they were members of a family, but because their status in the family was property owned by the head of the family. Which was not so different from the manner by which slaves were owned.'[1] In some cultures a child could be given as payment to a creditor. A girl might be given to cancel a debt, and she would become the mistress of the individual to whom she was given.

Feudalism in Europe was a hierarchical system which was believed to reflect on earth the hierarchy of heaven, with its archangels, angels and saints, and an omnipotent God at its apex. Social reconstructions of this belief in the arrangements of religious institutions, and the societies that evolved around them, have shown a remarkable persistence through time.

Veneration of the elderly, especially of men, had an even more direct significance in tribal societies where the hierarchy of the dead and living was blurred. The ancestors were closest to God and had to be propitiated in order to earn their goodwill towards the living. Among the living, the oldest members of the tribe, being close to death, had a privileged relationship to all those who had gone before. Ancestor worship was an extension into the supernatural of existing family structures, in which the older members enjoyed a high level of authority. The family comprised both the material world and the invisible, but no less real, world of the spirits. The family and the tribe transcended mortality, and the oldest were the bridge between the living and the dead.

Nor is this unintelligible to us. Even today, many people in the West think of the dead as 'looking down', 'watching over' the living, a mixture of guardian angel and moral police. The dead are granted the compensatory privilege of supervising our mortal lives. I was much struck, at the time of the death of Diana, Princess of Wales, by the number of cards and mementoes left by people outside Kensington Palace referring to her caring for people, and her ability to do so now from her place in heaven. Speaking ill of the dead remains a taboo, even if much weakened by a market avid for revelations and the true story of dead celebrities.

The idea of the patriarch, the paterfamilias, the head of family, has been remarkably tenacious in all castes and classes. Their power was not uncontested – the resentment it created in the young may be read in the almost universal severity of the laws against parricide. The next generation must have been often tempted to put an end to the tyranny of those who lived on, denying them their inheritance, land and the power that went with it. This temptation had to be limited by the threat of the most draconian punishments.

Nor was the power of the patriarch curbed by the coming of industrial society. Industrial discipline only strengthened the authority of senior males in all social classes, exemplified by the often tyrannical, though sometimes paternalistic, mill or factory owner. The industrial workers, who were at the mercy of the arbitrary power of employers, visited their own victimhood on those over whom they had control, their wives and children.

STATUS OF THE ELDERLY

Now, everywhere in the world, gerontocracy is dying, although faster in some cultures than others. In certain areas of the world, the weakening powers of the old have called forth a vigorous reaction and a sometimes violent reassertion of authority. This is one possible reading of the emergence of religious fundamentalism: the reclamation of traditional forms of social and spiritual control by priests, imams and all the other – usually aged – intermediaries between this world and the next. A reaffirmation of dominance expresses itself in a hardening of old faiths: fundamentalism, ostensibly 'a return to tradition', is a very contemporary phenomenon, a response to a modernisation which robs elders of power and undermines sources of authority.

In Africa, where rural, clan-based societies bestowed social and religious knowledge on elders, and where the main productive resource – land – was controlled by them, these patterns were first disrupted by colonialism. Later, Western-style education discredited ancient patterns of lordship by shamans, traditional healers and priests, and empowered those who had acquired the skills and knowledge appropriate to a new, urbanising and industrial society.

In Asia, joint and extended families are rapidly decaying under the same influences. The knowledge of the old is perceived increasingly as of dwindling use to, and an encroachment upon, the lives of a generation formed for a quite different way of living from anything known to their forebears. That the young should see this as liberation, and the elderly as evidence of deterioration, is scarcely surprising. But contemporary shifts in sensibility go far beyond a familiar cross-generational friction. They are symptomatic of more profound social and economic movements in the world, which have caught up whole cultures and civilisations in the compulsions of globalisation.

These have their origin in convulsive changes that have occurred in the West, where accelerating technological innovation, 'de-industrialisation' and economic restructuring have rapidly removed the skills and competences of an older generation in favour of the flexibility and adaptability of the young. The 'virtues' of frugality, thrift and self-denial have been eclipsed, since these are an embarrassment to a consumer society where status reflects spending power, and extravagance is a sign of success. Youth has acquired a social supremacy it has hitherto rarely enjoyed. This has been at the expense of the old.

LIFE EXPECTANCY AND GLOBALISATION

The dramatic rise in life expectancy is, to a considerable extent, a result of the application of medical technologies, which have prolonged life far beyond anything foreseen by the introduction of the welfare state in the mid-twentieth century. But in the rich countries, other factors have contributed to the rising proportion of elderly people, some of which are puzzling.

It was not anticipated that populations would fail to replenish themselves in the 'developed' world. In Britain, in 2002 the birth rate fell to 1.6, which is just below the level at which the population will maintain itself. Wolfgang Lutz of Austria's International Institute for Applied Systems Analysis estimates that almost half the population of Western Europe and Japan will be over 60 by the end of the twenty-first century.[2] This forecast may, of course, prove false, as demographic extrapolations often have been in the past. (There was, for instance, a scare in Britain in the 1930s about the future depopulation of the country. It was forecast then that the total population of Britain by 2000 would be a mere 35 million. This prediction was swiftly overtaken after the Second World War, when the birth rate rose again, affluence became widespread and, above all, young and healthy migrants from the Caribbean, India and Pakistan came to ease labour shortages, and in the process rejuvenated the population.) In spite of this, however, there is no doubt that a reduction in the proportion of people of working age in relation to the retired is imminent.

The social, economic and moral consequences of these developments are far-reaching, although there is by no means unanimity on their meaning. Some researchers find nothing disturbing in the projections. Professor Jane Falkingham of London School of Economics states, 'The number of pensioners tripled in the last century – from around 6 per cent in 1901 to 18 per cent in 2001 – and we coped with that without imploding.'[3] She foresees a rise in the number of over-60s to 25 per cent as 'manageable', although the 5 million over-80s expected by 2021 will place pressure on health services and social care. Optimists argue that with a healthier older population and their desire to go on working longer, with continuing economic growth and improving productivity, there is no reason for excessive concern.

Dr Gail Wilson is less sanguine.[4] She argues that globalisation endangers the collective social transfers that are essential to elders in later life, pointing out that work, the family and collective institutions are all jeopardised by the neo-liberal ideology that presently dominates the global economy: work is decreasingly available to older people in the West (despite the current talk of raising the retirement age), as well as in the South, as the informal economy is replacing a 'liberalised' formal sector; family support is eroded by growing individualism, while resistance to public spending is part of the global ideological curb on state provision for old age.

REPLACING THE GENERATIONS

The United States is the only industrialised country which has a fertility rate above the replacement level of 2.1 children per woman. The United States has also maintained a fairly steady flow of immigrants from all over the world. About 30 million people in the US were born outside the country, while there are an estimated 6 million undocumented migrants. These factors combine to protect the US against the threat of drastic population decline or a very high proportion of elderly. In spite of this, however, it is estimated that by 2020 23 per cent of the US population will be over 60. After the trauma of September 11, it may be that migration into the country will become more tightly controlled; the effect of this on the population profile and, consequently, on the dynamism and energy of the US is not yet clear.

In the US, the proportion of the population over 65 is expected to double by 2030 to 70 million, while the number of people over 80 will rise from 9.3 million in 2000 to 19.5 million in 2030. This will lead to increased health-care costs. In 1997, the US had the highest per capita health-care spending per person over 65 (US $12,100), by far greater than that of Canada (US $6,800) and the UK (US $3,600.) In the US, nursing home and home health-care spending doubled between 1990 and 2001, when it reached US $132 billion.

In North America, on average individuals between the ages of 65 and 69 have a further life expectancy of about 15 years. Between 75 and 79 it reaches ten years, and even at 80 it is six or seven years.

By 1996, in Canada 29 per cent of seniors lived alone, a figure that has grown steadily from 20 per cent in 1971. Between 1961 and 1991, the proportion of older women living alone more than doubled. These changes are due partly to shifting family structures and expectations, partly to the combination of widowhood and the higher average age among senior women in comparison with men, and partly to the greater independence that even a small pension, housing subsidies and community-based health-care supports make possible. Contrary to popular perception, the percentage of old people living in institutions and special-care homes has decreased from 10.2 per cent in 1971 to 7.3 per cent in 1996.[5] This pattern is in keeping with the experience of much of the developed world, and is a result of the closing of many state institutions such as geriatric wards and hospitals.

AGEISM

International agencies, governments, national charities and local organisations now routinely commit themselves to policies against ageism. These remain largely declaratory, although legislation against age discrimination in employment has been effective in the US, where the over-60s make up a larger proportion of the workforce than in any other Western country.

However this may be, the *social* power of the elderly shows little sign of being enhanced by their numbers. Youth, as an increasingly scarce commodity, is likely to go on appreciating in the demographic marketplace. If it has traditionally been the destiny of the young to rail against the authoritarianism and tyranny of age, there is little evidence that when the young are in the ascendant they are likely to be more merciful to their elders than these were to those subordinated to *them* in the past.

Nevertheless, the capacity to prolong life yet further, into the tenth and eleventh decade, is constantly advertised by enthusiasts of technological progress. These promises of a provisional immortality are limited only by questions sometimes raised about the purpose and function of superfluous aged populations, their unproductiveness and their dead weight on the declining number of earners of the future. It seems we are likely to hear much more about the desirability – or otherwise – of shortening, rather than extending, the lifespan by a further 20 years. Certainly, Dr Lutz foresees what he calls, perhaps somewhat delicately, 'intergenerational political conflict'. In this context, the discussions on euthanasia now taking place in Europe have an ominous undertone.

THE YOUTH OF MIGRANTS

In 1950, in Britain there were six workers for every pensioner. Today the ratio is four to one. By the middle of the twenty-first century, this will fall to 2.4 to one, unless there is *further immigration*. It is clear that the changing demography of the country has profound repercussions on every area of life. It cannot be treated reductively or in isolation from the great movements of population in the world set in train by globalisation.

The governments of Europe are now in the unhappy position of trying to appease the far right, which has successfully linked the sense of insecurity of the people with xenophobia and racism. At the same time, they must manage a deficit of youth in their society as well as labour shortages in crucial areas of the economy, notably, medical and welfare services, teaching, information technology and the tourism industry.

A spokesman for the racist British National Party suggested that the policies of the mainstream political parties amounted to a 'genocide' of the British people.[6] He stated that the immigration policies of the government were creating a threat, whereby the number of youthful incomers of childbearing age and with a high birth rate would lead to whites being outnumbered by non-whites 'within 60 years'. The hysteria engendered in recent years by the perception of 'asylum seekers', particularly those believed to be 'bogus', has made it harder to renew an ageing population by welcoming vigorous and healthy young people from elsewhere. The right has appropriated discussion, by the use of words like 'swamp' or 'flood' or 'stemming the tide', so that migrants now come to appear like an unstoppable force of nature: the language of natural catastrophe is employed to conceal the reality of a disaster of wholly human making.

That this is against our own self-interest is barely acknowledged by political leaders. Their evasions have led to some puzzling and contradictory actions. They want to be seen conspicuously deporting 'illegal' migrants, while at the same time recruiting – sometimes in countries from which deportees have come – nurses, doctors, veterinary personnel, people qualified in information technology, as well as workers for the catering industry and seasonal agricultural workers. This may relieve some pressure on the labour market, but it is unlikely to redress demographic imbalances.

The implications are grave. Without a more ample and permissive opening of borders, the countries of Europe may find themselves overwhelmingly populated by the middle-aged and elderly, without enough active young people to pay for the pensions systems and care on which they will depend. It might well be wondered why anyone would hesitate if it were a choice between an ethnically and age-diverse population and a country of frail but pure white elders with no one to look after them.

WHO ARE THE ELDERLY?

Apocalyptic predictions are very much in the millennial air – resource depletion, global warning, pollution, the 'clash of civilisations', terrorism. It is perhaps salutary to bear in mind once more the arguments against the scare of a 'greying population'. Improvements in the health of the elderly have been quite easily achieved in Britain: the proportion of men and women at any particular age who require help with four basic activities in daily living halved between 1976 and 1991.[7] This suggests that people will become dependent only much later in life than has until recently been the case. 'Active ageing' is now the slogan, maintaining health, fitness and mobility until late in life. In any case, the median age of the people of Britain will rise only from 38 to 44 in the next 40 years, which scarcely suggests cataclysmic change. (In 1901 the median age was 24, in 1931 30, and in 1981 almost 35.) Everything depends upon whether we place our faith in economic growth continuing as it has done for the past 25 years, or whether we believe that the demographic predictions will prove a more decisive determinant on future well-being.

In any case, even definitions of the elderly are changing. Old age is not a chronological given, although for the purposes of the administration of social benefits it may be necessary to impose it. We are now seeing *a different kind of elderly*. Efforts to maintain health, both physical and mental, to attend carefully to diet and exercise, and to remain engaged participants in the life of society are changing the sensibility and psyche of the older person. Society may be slow to appreciate the transformation of attitudes and outlook of the elderly, but they have undergone a metamorphosis no less profound than that which changed young people into the previously unheard-of category of teenagers in the 1950s. The change in the elderly might not be so glamorous, but it is unlikely to be reversed. There isn't a word for this new – and possibly, transient – class; perhaps we might call them the *gilderly*.

THE COST OF AGEING

Britain, it is often argued, is better placed than most other countries in Europe to keep down the costs of sustaining its future elderly, mainly because of the extreme modesty of the state old age pension. This represents a mere 16 to 18 per cent of the average national wage. If it remains at that level there is no reason why, even with a growing population of pensioners, the cost should rise much above the existing level of 5 per cent of GDP. This will present no problem. The more generous pensions provided by the state in Germany, France and the Netherlands will absorb between 14 and 18 per cent of GDP of those countries within 30 years. This is a far more onerous commitment.

This is the optimistic view. But if employment falters, if the low-wage service economy permits little or no savings to millions of people, if other kinds of ill-health affect the elderly, what then? In what other form will the state subsidise extreme old age and infirmity so that this is not a time of penny-pinching misery and want, as it remains for about one-third of pensioners today?

The projected rise in the number of elderly over the next two generations is unlikely to be reversed. Hoping for the best is a risky policy in any area of governance, and when it comes to taking care of the weak and most vulnerable it would be negligent to rely upon economic growth in perpetuity, upon the goodwill of future generations or even upon the capacity of private pension schemes to ensure the financial stability of the old. The precautionary principle ought to apply in this case, no less than in that of global warming or any other sign of potential breakdown in social, ecological or economic order.

REPLENISHING THE POPULATION

What is certain is that, within little more than a generation, the population of much of the developed world will be ageing and falling. It will also be fat (more than 20 per cent are expected to be obese). These mutations in European society are unparalleled in modern times, and it is scarcely surprising that the policies to deal with them are both improvised and inadequate.

What does it mean, if rich societies fail to replenish themselves? Have they become too – what? – selfish? frightened? liberated? Does it matter? Are declining populations a blessing to the crowded lands of Japan or the Netherlands? Has child-bearing become too burdensome? Should we celebrate the freedom of women from an ancient cycle of pregnancy and childbirth, subservience and enslavement to the will of men? What are the consequences of elective childlessness for the future structure and cohesion of society?

Or have children simply become too expensive? In the United States, where most aspects of human life have been meticulously costed, the Department of Agriculture estimates that it now costs between US $121,000 and US $241,000 to bring up a child. A baby born today will be even more costly. By the age of 17, these omnivorous infants will have devoured between US $171,000 and US $340,000. It seems that the privileged people of the world are coming to regard children as something of a luxury. The comfort of the present depends not only upon growing inequality in the distribution of the wealth of the world, but is also constructed on the absence of the unborn. How future – and possibly depleted – generations will regard the legacy bequeathed by their begetters scarcely troubles a world which feels the pressing problems of today weigh upon it quite heavily enough without having to think about those of a distant tomorrow.

THE WEST AND THE REST

The Western model of development has now usurped all others and is presented as the sole source of hope and renewal to the whole world. What are the implications of this, when it creates a Japan or an Italy peopled by shadows, whose lives have been prolonged by technology far beyond anything that can be understood as their 'natural term'? What will these people do, sitting in the low-watt penumbra of old-age homes, their hearing ruined by decades of hyper-decibel music, their eyesight dimmed by long years of voyeuristic television, their memories all but erased by the media-crowded images of the day before yesterday? Even in the West such an achievement chills the spirit. Can it be, should it be, exported globally?

In its example to the world of abstention from increasing its population, we have a rare case of Europe and Japan practising what they preach – a birth control so effective that we can see future generations dwindling before our eyes. In the meantime, it is clear that the people of the rich countries will be able to ransack the countries of the South for urgently needed personnel to service our dereliction. Having already extracted maximum profit from their crop lands, forests, seas and mineral riches, and having taken advantage of the cheapness of their labour in the slums of Mexico City, Jakarta and Dhaka, we shall now pluck out the people they depend on most to help their own countries deal with the asperities of globalisation – doctors and nurses, carers for the old and infirm. Of course, people-stealing is not new. It was once known as slavery, but in the transformed circumstances of globalisation, this now appears as privilege.

* * *

This book reflects upon some of these unresolved questions. In the West, will an ageing population be sufficiently robust and healthy to contribute to the prosperity of the economy, or will it place intolerable strains on both services and society? In the South, can the rising numbers of elderly be absorbed by the traditional social safety nets of family, or will industrialisation rob them of that security without the compensations of adequate pensions and health care? In the great drama of globalisation, are the growing populations of elderly gainers or losers? Are we confronted by a 'demographic time bomb' or an unparalleled opportunity to make use of the experience and knowledge of the years?

Chapter 1

ISSUES ON AGEING

In her study, *Old Age*,[1] Simone de Beauvoir mentions three distinct issues that have to be confronted. The first is the subjective, sometimes overwhelming, realisation that one has become old, with all that implies in terms of individual anxiety and fear. This is the existential aspect of ageing – how it is borne in upon us, how we come to terms with it, how we resist or are reconciled to the inevitable. The second is the variety of ways in which old age is mediated by the different societies and cultures on earth: these range from treating old age as a culmination of fulfilment and wisdom, to regarding it as a time of uselessness and futility; or, more usually, some combination of these. The third is the question for 'developed' societies of the policies, institutions and structures required to deal with the growing population of the elderly. In the generation since de Beauvoir was writing, we might add a fourth – the increasing numbers of elderly in poor societies. The West grew rich before it grew old. The South is in the process of growing old before it has become rich.

BECOMING OLD

Ageing seems to take most people by surprise. The individual experiences life as continuous, and there are no rites of passage, no ceremonies, no rituals to mark entrance into old age. Traditionally, the menopause was such a moment for women; within living memory, in Europe women went into black soon after they had ceased childbearing. I remember my grandmother as a woman in black satin skirt, black boots, a black astrakhan coat, a black hat, and carrying a black handbag. No such event signalled to men that they had passed the invisible frontier; although the institution of 'retirement' signalled the end of a publicly defined function.

One of the paradoxes of ageing is that we become someone else while still remaining ourselves. The outer transformation is difficult to accommodate, even in the most favourable circumstances, when health and vitality remain in spite of the years.

> I was astonished one day when a young woman took my arm as I was crossing the road. I thought she was going to steal my handbag or something. But she smiled at me, and I knew she had perceived me as an elderly person in need of help. I was shocked and troubled. I went home and looked at myself in the mirror. I thought, I am still myself, but that self is no longer apparent to other people. Then I began to wonder, Was it ever apparent to other people? Are we not always alone with our own subjective experience? Are even our relationships as young people perhaps not always dances between shadows, in which the energy and bloom of youth create the illusion of connecting? Of course I didn't dwell on these things, but they all occurred to me for the first time when I was in my late 60s. (Woman, 80, South London)

In 2002, I met Ivy, who, at the age of 79, had fallen in the street one day when she was hurrying to catch a bus. She said:

> I fell flat on my face. I was bleeding from the head, and I was dazed more than anything. People were very kind, but a crowd soon gathered. I heard one young woman say, 'Poor old thing.' I thought afterwards, Yes, love, you were right three times. I am poor. I am old. And, above all, I am a thing. That's how they look at you.

People often say you're as young as you feel. They are, perhaps, trying to bridge the mysterious gulf between their own constant idea of who they are and other people's changed behaviour towards them. To be elderly is to lead a double life, to be a kind of secret agent, an emissary of the time to come, a spy from another world: the rooted self that is unchanging coexists with the social mask of the aged person to which others increasingly respond. Many people speak of old age with exasperation, angry that it disguises their enduring reality and disturbs the subjective sense of continuity which their own internal life provides them with.

Many elderly people prefer to think of themselves as sick rather than old. Illness is a metaphor for old age, and may dissimulate the advancing years behind the symptoms of illness. The reduced quality of life brought about by failing bodily and mental powers is often felt as an assault upon identity. Others embrace illness as legitimising a retreat from the world. My mother, late in life, turned to illness not merely as a source of identity (she was never happier than when she was in hospital, which she contrived to be with increasing frequency), but as a companion and consolation. Her illness became inseparable from her, a source of endless contemplation and anxious interrogation. She communed with the sickness within and withdrew from communication with others. Whenever I visited her she would speak of it tenderly, with affection even, as though it had become her real child or a pampered pet. I often felt my presence was an intrusion on their privacy.

While some people prefer to be sick than old, others use old age as an alibi, not only for infirmity, but for depression, a sense of disappointment or loss, or more diffuse feelings of ill-being. It is common to plead old age rather than admit to more serious sickness, and in this case it may become a form of denial. As my neighbour grew thinner and visibly deteriorated, he ascribed it to his age until, ravaged by cancer, he collapsed. He died within a couple of weeks of being admitted to hospital. Simone de Beauvoir says, 'The notion of disease is exorcised by calling upon age; that of age by summoning up disease. And by means of this alternation it becomes possible to believe neither in the one nor the other.'[2]

On the other hand, some people invoke old age before they reach it. It can serve as a haven for dissatisfaction or regret; an asylum for bitterness or rejection. People are often said to 'let themselves go' when they no longer expect anything of life. Self-neglect, the disruption of the daily pattern of existence, failure to eat properly – all may be a result of the ebbing of energy, particularly among those who are left alone by the loss of a partner. Old age may be used to demand privilege or sympathy, although today this is a wasting asset – there is too much competition for it to be very effective.

Emotions do not change, despite appearances. The most common complaint of older people is that they are patronised, infantilised or ignored. For some, it comes as a relief that they no longer have to worry about what kind of impression they will make, and that they do not have to tolerate people they do not like. Time, they often say, is too short to waste on social niceties:

one reason why many older people are seen as irascible or cantankerous is that they increasingly dispense with formality and do not conceal what they really think or want. 'We become more like ourselves' is the common reaction – characteristics we have had all our lives become more pronounced.

The customary markers of the passage into old age have been, in industrial society, retirement and grandparenthood. Both of these have become more fluid in a world where work is less structured, where people change jobs regularly and fewer people pursue a lifelong career. The pattern of ceremonial leave-taking from the firm or company, the badge of service, the watch or carriage clock have all but disappeared. In any case, the definition of an age at which people should retire is dictated more by a need to set an age at which pensions should be paid rather than by the readiness of individuals to withdraw from the workforce. In 1909, the retirement age was fixed at 70. It was reduced to 65 in 1928, and to 60 for women in 1941.

> Retirement is a relatively recent phenomenon. In industrialized countries in the 1930s, between 40 and 70 per cent of all men aged 65 and over were working for pay. By 1971 the proportion of aged men doing paid work in Canada had declined markedly to 25 per cent, and by 1988 that number had fallen to 10.3 per cent. In the 1920s and 1930s one elderly woman in five was working for a wage, but by 1998 this had shrunk to less than one in thirty.[3]

In recent decades, many people have left full-time employment well before the official retirement age, and others work on in part-time jobs, doing work that bears no relation to an earlier career. In the 1990s in Britain, about half of men between 55 and 59, and two-thirds of those between 60 and 64 were not working. This, to some extent, does away with the external signals that tell people that they have now become old. Rest, as a reward for years of labour, often seems a savourless prospect for those who still have the energy and power to work.

> 'He doesn't know what to do with himself,' said the wife of a retired steelworker. 'He does the allotment. He has his pigeons. But they're not a full-time job. He was laid off at 58, there was nothing wrong with him. But there is now. I've watched him

> go downhill. It grieves me, it does. And it also gets on my nerves. I can't stand to have him around the house. He follows me about. It's vexing. I lose my temper with him sometimes, then I could bite my tongue off for being so unkind. We have enough money, it isn't that. But he was working at 15 and he's never known anything else. He used to go to the pub with his mates, I wish he would now. But he says retired people have got nothing in common except time on their hands.'

Nor does the birth of grandchildren necessarily present the irrefutable evidence that a new generation may have formerly provided, that you are, indeed, old. There are many reasons for this, not the least being the scattering of families, the moving away from home, the work that has summoned children away to distant towns or even countries. I have often been struck, in the living rooms of elderly people, by the number of pictures of kinsfolk no longer present. 'That's my mother and father,' they'll say, 'she was a saint and he treated her really badly. That's my sister and me at the fair one Easter Monday. That's my daughter when she graduated, and the one over there is my son in America. These are the grandchildren. He's doing ever so well for himself, she's at university doing business studies, whoever heard of such things? That's me and my brother the first time we ever went abroad. Spain. Of course, they say, they visit when they can, but they have a lot of responsibilities and they lead such busy lives – there is ballet and football, and she is learning the flute and he is going on a school journey, they can't be running about after me every five minutes.' And they point to the telephone, the lifeline, the cord that links them to those they love. One old woman said to me:

> When we were young we were close. The family all lived in the same streets in the Pear Tree area. Every few days you just went to see each other. Not that you had much to say. They used to open the door, shout up the passageway and walk in. My auntie used to say, 'I thought I'd come and have a look at you.' That's what she did, literally. They went to look at each other; and they would know at a glance if somebody was off colour, out of sorts, was worried about a lump that had come, or a husband who was playing away...

In any case, grandparents are no longer necessarily old. The perception which many older people have of the depletion of families is justified. They were used to crowded households (the average household in Britain today consists of 2.3 people). Childhoods in the early twentieth century were peopled by siblings, cousins, aunts and uncles. Families were extended laterally. Today's families are constructed differently, extended vertically, so that four or five generations remain in contact.

Marie is a grandmother at 34. Her 16-year-old daughter, Tiffany, has just given birth. Marie's own mother and grandmother are both still alive. Tiffany was still at school, but she left when the baby was born. After a few weeks, she became bored and got a job in a pharmacy. She left the baby to Marie, who said that she felt like a young mother again. It reminded her of the time when Tiffany was a baby and she was living with her boyfriend, a brief time of happiness before he left her.

Tiffany enjoys her life and wants to go out in the evenings, so she leaves the baby, Jessica, increasingly in her mother's care. Marie sometimes leaves the baby with her mother, Pat. Pat, in her 50s, is working part-time, so there are days when this is not convenient for her. Pat's own mother, Enid, is in her mid-70s, badly crippled with arthritis, but delighted to take care of baby Jessica from time to time.

Marie puts her foot down. 'You cannot pass that child around like a parcel. Enid is too old, you're taking advantage of her.' 'No, she loves it.' Tiffany moves in with her boyfriend, who is 28, already twice married, but he has children of his own and doesn't want any more kids around. Marie agrees to bring up Jessica. She gives up her own job – ironically, in a nursing home for the elderly – but she soon misses the company, and returns to work. She pays Pat to look after the baby during the hours she is working.

Baby Jessica is cared for. Between them, four generations do the work which might formerly have been carried out by brothers and sisters, aunts and uncles, cousins. The vertically integrated family is as competent as the laterally extended family. Jessica, now four, is a healthy child, and will start school next year. She calls all the adults around her by their first name. None, not even her mother, is known by her role.

> The four generations of women are very close. They live within two or three miles of each other. They quarrel from time to time: they compete with each other for importance in the baby's life. But they see one another most days. Enid, although handicapped, remains the matriarch. She deplores the girls' (as she calls them) inability to stay with their men. She remained with her husband until he died ten years ago, even though, as she says, 'I loved him but I never liked him.' Enid says she has no sense of growing old. She is cared for and respected.

There are no precedents for our becoming old, however closely we may have observed it in others. It is an individual experience, and people make of it what they can, according to their material means and inner resources. It can be bewildering, and when they become weakened or sick, some people express resentment, as though age itself were a form of discrimination, an arbitrary visitation upon them, particularly while *so many people remain young*. For most of us, it dawns slowly, progressively. You notice people overtaking you when you walk briskly along the pavement. Everyone else on the underground is younger. Someone offers you a seat. People look away when they catch your eye – a glance indicates that you have ceased to be a sexual object. At the checkout, someone is drumming their fingers on the counter while you look for coins in your purse. You fall asleep in the chair and when you wake, it is dark and you are for a moment disoriented; you call out the name of a dead husband, an absent child. How silly I have become, it's five o'clock and now I shan't sleep all night. You forget an appointment, and when the telephone rings at an unexpected time, your heart beats uncontrollably. Who can that be? And you don't answer the doorbell after dark, for fear of the bogus officials and council inspectors who might rob your pension. You start to hide things, even though no one knows where they are, not even yourself when you look for the pension book or the cheque that came in the post. And you find yourself thinking more and more about the past – a subject so absorbing that the present is colonised by its compelling power, and you can scarcely remember what happened yesterday. The days become mysteriously long, and the years short: time recently consumed is ashes, but the significant events of long ago are preserved perfectly, luminous, in perpetual clarity. Awareness is borne in upon us gradually, so that – in theory – we have time to get used to the idea.

But we have only just accustomed ourselves to being who we are! And that is someone in the prime of life! We only recently gained confidence to be ourselves. We have only just come to terms with our own limitations, the realisation that we will not reach the ambitions we had conceived for ourselves, we shall never do all the things we wanted; we have made our peace with the relationships we have formed, the family or partnership of which we are a part; and then, it seems we have to accommodate ourselves to this new, incredible reality! Soon it will all be over. Somewhere deep inside, we do not believe it. It is a terrible masquerade. Someone will tell us everything is all right. When we dream, we are no longer old, the hills are not getting steeper, we are restored to our vigour and youth, we revisit an undiminished energy. Surely that is the person I truly am. Here are the photographs to prove it: that is me, among the group of young people at a twenty-first birthday party. This is the real person, the authentic me; even though I have learned so much since then, I feel pity for that innocent who knew nothing of future responsibility and loss!

We look at our siblings, our peers, our friends and resent them for looking so much older. Why did you lose your hair, why does your stomach bulge, what happened to your figure? Why these absences in the conversation, why can't you remember the word, what are you on about? And we want to blame them for their own culpable negligence when only time has passed its withering hand over them. But who can protest against time, that inexorable abstraction? What you can do is quarrel with real flesh and blood, its slowing tempo and fading power. And irritation is succeeded by tenderness for those with whom we have grown old, and we have a foreboding of loss. Who will die first? Whose funeral will be the next in the lengthening list of those who have gone? And anyway, who wants to live on into their 90s when this is such a lonely experience? You find yourself apologising for your own longevity, and the children say, 'Don't be silly, Mum, I don't know what I'd do without you,' although you notice how they glance at the clock and say they must be off, even though it seems they have only just arrived.

My own mother died in 1990 in a nursing home. She was immobilised, partly by Parkinson's but also by fear and agoraphobia. She could do nothing for herself in the end and depended on others to feed her, dress her and take her to the toilet. She would become dehydrated because she didn't like to ask the agency night staff to take her to the toilet. It is a curious thing that, even when we are still emotionally very close to the old, they remain, as it were, in a different world of infirmity and enfeeblement: however deep the bond of kinship and love, they are alien to us; just as the aged people that we, in our turn, if we survive, will become are strangers to the young or middle-aged individuals we are. We cannot know. We cannot anticipate. Sometimes you recognise characteristics you share with a parent or close relative, and you have an intuitive understanding, 'Yes, that is how I will become.'

This is what I wrote after one visit to my mother in her nursing home:

> Sometimes when I went to see her, she would be sitting in the public lounge. It was impossible to remain unaware of the social function of those cramped circles of high-backed chairs around the walls, the Zimmer frames, the persistent odour of urine and disinfectant, the television playing Australian soap opera, while heads fall forward on wasted chests, and hands continue to work away as though still at the bench or lathe they had abandoned 20 years earlier. For their fate is our future: the effect upon us of their immobility, of their confusion and helplessness is to make us realise how short the time is, and how we must hurry, hurry, to live life to the full in the brief years that stand between us and the catatonic stillness of the afternoon hours, when the summer breeze inhabits the net curtains and the geraniums blaze in their hanging baskets, and the old people sleep their shallow after-dinner sleep.[4]

We are all alone with our own ageing. We shall doubtless meet it according to the kind of person we have been; but even that may offer a slender enough guide, for who knows what other person we may become when confronted by physical loss, mental failure or emotional dereliction?

A study of old age in Canada suggests it is marked by at least four significant assumptions: *separation*: that old people are a special group whose unique problems separate them from the rest of society; *hidden*: the experience and plight of the elderly, far from being taken into account by society, somehow remain 'out of sight' and hidden from view; *dependent*: because they may be in need of some help, the ageing lose their right to independence; *useless*: old people have no useful purpose and are a drain on society's resources. These myths are tenacious and incapacitating. They reach deeply into a culture which values living in the present, hedonism and immediacy above reflection, experience and the growth of wisdom.[5]

HOW SOCIETIES DEAL WITH AGEING

Most of the ambiguous and contradictory feelings aroused in individuals by their growing old have been expressed socially by one culture or another at some time. When the old retain control of resources, they maintain their power. When they are keepers of secrets, have magical powers, are intermediaries between the living and the dead, they are respected, even feared. When they have experience indispensable for survival, they are objects of veneration and solicitude. In subsistence economies – and that means most of them during recorded history – the knowledge of the old was vital to survival. If they have come through seasons when harvests failed and they know where to find the roots and berries of starvation foods, if they have overcome adversity or war, have learned to hide themselves in the forest, or make shelters in the jungle, what they know will be of profound interest to a new generation. Even in industrial society, for as long as poverty and want remained constant companions of the families of workers, knowing how to make and mend, to contrive and scheme, to make a meal out of next to nothing, were skills to hand on to children, eager for instruction in ways of providing for *their* family when the time came. When this form of poverty receded, the tradition faded; knowledge and power were taken out of the hands and memories of the old, and growing affluence stranded them in a place which a new generation hoped never to visit again, and accordingly their power diminished. This is, perhaps, the key to a widespread subjective feeling among old people that they are neglected: it is simply that their role in cross-generational transmission of values has decayed.

Some societies, particularly those habitually so close to subsistence that every unproductive person becomes a burden, may deal very harshly indeed with those who can no longer work. This becomes the definition of old age: when he or she can no longer contribute to the labour necessary for survival. Simone de Beauvoir states,

> Among the Hopi, the Creek and Crow Indians, and the Bushmen of South Africa, it was customary to lead the aged person to a hut specially built for the purpose away from the village, and there to abandon him, leaving a little food and water. The Eskimo, whose resources are meagre and most uncertain, persuade the old to go and lie in the snow and wait for death; or they forget them on an ice-floe when the tribe is out fishing... It was usual for the Amassalik Eskimo in Greenland to kill themselves when they felt they were a burden to the community.[6]

On the other hand,

> ...among the Aleut the fate of the old is happy... The Aleuts move in canoes and live by fishing – whale meat and fermented fish-heads. Tough and resistant, they sometimes go days on end without eating. They do not accumulate possessions but have prodigious memories. They practise shamanism. If the Aleut treats his parents well and if he attends to their advice, he will be rewarded: his fishing will be good and he will live to be old. Living to be old means providing the later generations with a great example. The very old men teach the young: every village used to have one or two elders who instructed the children; they were listened to carefully, even if they wandered in their speech.[7]

The Inuit indigenous people of Northern Canada have no word for 'senior citizen'.[8]

The two extremes – of abandonment of the old and extreme veneration of them – are not incompatible, even within the same society. While the vigorous and healthy elderly may well be deferred to, heeded and respected, when they become ill and frail and it is time for them to die, they may be abandoned or expected to remove themselves from those who must go on living. This is not necessarily cruel. If it is a known and customary fate for the enfeebled to be left to their inevitable death, then it is simply normal social practice, embedded in the culture. The elderly are resigned to it, and will co-operate with the rituals which will hasten their end.

In general, Simone de Beauvoir concludes,

> We may infer that the most usual choice of inadequate resources, whether they are agricultural or nomadic, is to sacrifice the old… When a society has a certain margin of security, there seems on the face of it to be a reasonable supposition that it will maintain its aged people; it is in the adults' interest to look to their own future.[9]

The conflicting feelings that hover around the old in any society are crystallised in what ageing presages – fear of death. In *Science, Magic and Religion*,[10] Malinowski says,

> Of all sources of religion, the supreme and final crisis of life – death – is of the greatest importance. Death is the gateway to the other world in more than the literal sense… Man has to live his life in the shadow of death, and he who clings to life in all its fullness must read the menace of its end. And he who is faced by death turns to the promise of life. Death and its denial – immortality – have always formed, as they form today, the most poignant theme of man's forebodings. The extreme complexity of man's emotional reactions to life finds necessarily its counterpart in his attitude to death… Even among the most primitive peoples, the attitude towards death is infinitely more complex and, I may add, more akin to our own, than is usually assumed.

Few cultures regard death as final, even though loss of the living most certainly is. And in our time, the decay of faith in an afterlife has certainly fed the almost mystical dedication to the cult of living (the idea of life lived to the full, crammed with as many experiences, sensations and distractions as possible), has created a genuinely new kind of society in which eternity must be mined in the temporal rather than deferred to some future or afterlife. This sets up its own pathologies, to which we shall return.

The old, then, occupy a unique position, but it is as shifting and fugitive as life itself, and as full of contradictions. The old have secrets. They know what went on before the birth of the majority of people alive today. They are thus twice removed from us, closer both to what went before and separated from what is to come only by the thinnest membrane. On the other hand, they have ceased to produce. They cannot weed or hoe the fields or stand ankle-deep in the water of the paddy fields. Ultimately, they can no longer even perform light domestic chores, like preparing vegetables, cleaning vessels or washing clothes. Their physical and mental enfeeblement soon turns them into a burden in societies living close to the margin of survival.

Their magical powers, occupying as they do the penumbra between the living and the dead, may be a malign or a beneficent force. Sometimes, the dead become ghosts, and they often continue to be numbered among the members of the family group or tribe, so that death becomes only a faint discontinuity in the history of the group. In many societies, elders become members of a supreme controlling body or council; they have the right to make sacrifices to the gods or ancestral spirits, to exorcise devils and erase impurities. Those who believe in reincarnation sometimes claim to recognise the presence of those who have died in the newborn. (This happens not only in societies remote from the West. The idea of 'reincarnation' has taken popular root in the West. I spoke recently with a woman whose grandmother had died on the day before the birth of her child. She knew that her grandmother's spirit had entered the body of the newborn.)

There is something a little schematic in this formulation. There is no doubt a powerful relationship between the material margin of survival of any society and attitudes towards the elderly, but it is not a kind of natural law. The testimony of those who have lived and entered into the spirit of other societies tells another story. Helena Norberg-Hodge who spent 25 years observing how the Buddhist society of Ladakh in Jammu and Kashmir first came into contact with, and was influenced by, the modern world, has this to say of the old:

> Old people participate in all spheres of life. For the elderly in Ladakh, there are no years of staring into space, unwanted and alone; they are important members of the community until the day they die. Old age implies years of valuable experience and wisdom. Grandparents are not so strong, but they have

> other qualities to contribute; there is no hurry to life, so if they work more slowly, it does not matter. They remain a part of the family and community, so active that even in their 80s, they are usually fit and healthy, their minds clear. One of the main reasons why old people remain so alive and involved is their constant contact with the young.[11]

Cultures in which technological change is slow will naturally respect tradition. As changes in production accelerate, the old are often overtaken and robbed of social purpose. Many look with longing on traditional, static cultures, where it was the duty of young people simply to replicate the way of life of a previous generation with minimal disruption or change – it was their purpose to absorb the rituals that would ensure the rains would come, to enact the rites of passage that would enable them to become adults, and to listen to stories of the old, which constituted the memory, lore and identity of the group. Significantly, Norberg-Hodge called her book *Ancient Futures*. She is suggesting that inspiration for human survival should be sought in those which do not abuse the resource base upon which they, like all human cultures and civilisations, depend for survival. Those broken cultures cannot be restored, mended or recovered; but the values they embody may serve as a source of future hope.

There is no question, then, of 'returning' to more integrated societies where the elderly were the repository of knowledge, power or magic. It is possible to discern in these *ageing*, and even *dying* societies, however, principles other than those of rigorous age stratification and market-driven peer groups which govern the 'advanced' societies. It is conceivable that more harmonious inter-generational relationships might be possible, in a more generous society than that dominated by hierarchies of youth, money and celebrity.

Ruth Benedict, in *Patterns of Culture,*[12] recalls a conversation she had with an old man in California, a chief of those known as the Digger Indians. 'In the beginning,' he said, 'God gave to every people a cup, a cup of clay, and from this cup they drank their life.' He went on, 'They all dipped in the water, but their cups were different. Our cup has broken now. It has passed away.' Ruth Benedict observes,

> These things that had given significance to the life of his people, the domestic rituals of eating, the obligations of the economic system, the succession of ceremonials in the villages, possessions in the bear dance, their standard of right and wrong – these were gone, and with them, the shape and meaning of their lives... He did not mean that there was any question of the extinction of his peoples. But he had in mind the loss of something that had value equal to that of life itself, the whole fabric of his people's standards and beliefs.

As with cultures, so it is with people.

AGEING IN THE RICH WORLD

The myths we construct around old age are of greatest use to active young people, who do not want to linger or think too deeply on the fate that awaits all who survive. This is why it is important to look, not at official ideologies of ageing, but at the way old people are actually treated by society. No politician in the West is going to say that the old are an obstacle to economic progress, a dead weight on the young; a humanitarian rectitude would prevent any such declaration, but this may be how it appears, as deeper attitudes inevitably emerge to colour and permeate policies. Similarly, societies which appear to neglect the old, apparently abandon them or leave them to die in isolation may simply be expressing the urgency of survival of the group, with which the old willingly comply.

The sentimental Western image of the death of an old person, of a loving family gathered around the deathbed of a loved parent, smoothing the brow and holding the hand as the revered one breathes her or his last, has become rare. There is an increasing likelihood of people dying in hospital. With one in three people now living alone in Britain (the majority of them widowed, people who insist they do not want to leave the familiar environment), some die alone; and it is not uncommon to hear stories of neighbours alerted to the disappearance of the individual, not by her or his absence, but by the smell emanating from behind the locked door. This occurs relatively infrequently, but it has become emblematic of what is seen as a growing indifference to the fate of the elderly. Indeed, the great majority of lone old people are cared for by their children or siblings, and this image of dying alone is probably best read as a metaphor for something else; namely, the disengagement between the generations, the social rather than the emotional distance that has grown between them.

It is always difficult to distinguish between the biological process, the existential inevitability of ageing, and the social expression of this. Yet it is important to do so; for to regard it as a consequence of 'fate' is to invite helplessness and even neglect; while, on the other hand, deploying all the technology available in order to maintain the life of those no longer enhanced by it may divert resources and effort from where these might be more fruitfully used. The balance between what is possible and what is fitting is a very delicate one. It surfaces in the question of 'rationing' health care for the elderly: certain exclusions become necessary, withholding some of the increasingly expensive high technology of survival from those least likely to benefit from it. Many elderly people recognise this and sometimes prepare for it by requesting that they should not be resuscitated if medical treatment fails.

Age must always mean loss, particularly beyond a certain time, which is not chronological, but is experienced by the individual according to her or his health, well-being, level of social participation and quality of relationships. The decline of strength and power, growing dependency on others, anxiety, not so much about death itself as about the manner of dying, are rarely interpreted as welcome or positive events. What can be said, however, is that certain groups are less likely to be overwhelmed by the fear of death than others. Research suggests that men worry about death as the annihilation of their achievements, while women dwell more upon the severing of emotional and affective ties with others. The young, as always, believe they are immortal. Those most prey to fears of death and dying are the middle-aged; it seems that many over 55 are less oppressed, having, perhaps, come to terms with it. There is little evidence that old age is a time of serenity, reconciliation, acceptance, an asexual and sanitised antechamber of eternity: this is essentially a construct of those as yet untroubled by their own future extinction.

The denial of death, understandable in youth, has, in the past two generations, also affected many older people themselves. The age at which people admit to growing older has risen. People in their 60s regularly now refer to themselves as middle-aged. At the recent funeral of an aged friend, of whose life I wrote a celebration, her daughter objected to the passage that suggested her children had grown old: she insisted that I replaced the word 'old' with 'mature years'. She was herself 66.

This same friend died after a long and healthy life. She was in her 90s, and spent ten days in hospital before she died. As her relatives gathered at her bedside, she clearly expressed the trouble in her spirit at leaving them. So preoccupied are we with the guilt of those left behind (Did I do enough, could I have prevented it, did I say often enough I love you?) that I had never previously thought about the guilt of the dying. Yet that, too, has to be accommodated. She was begging her children for permission to die. This they wisely gave, and she did not survive for many days after that.

* * *

The role of elders has changed dramatically in the rich industrial societies. The idea of the self subordinated to a chain of familial continuity has been supplanted by that of the supremacy of the individual. The social function of people has altered too, especially that of men whose identity is now less determined by what they do, by their contribution to the work of society. Today we serve economic purposes which reward us as individuals. A (substantial) minority have well-defined careers in professional or managerial hierarchies, but, for most, work has become arbitrary and incidental: flexibility and adaptability are the key words. People must be ready for whatever new economic purpose they may be called upon – sometimes briefly – to fulfil. The self is now expressed principally not through cultural inheritance and customary practice, but by means of 'buying in' all that is necessary for a full life. Such developments are bound to have repercussions on the sense of purpose of generations formed for a quite different society, where people were defined by labour, social class and belonging. Being and having are more central to the culture than doing; and this is shocking to people who had grown up with discipline, self-denial and labour.

In the light of these changed circumstances, it is perhaps only natural that the old should make great efforts to prolong youth, to retain mobility, to participate fully in the consumer society, to which many of them have come late in life. In some ways, this is a positive development. The memory of the time when women went into perpetual mourning at the time of the menopause was a sadly reductive expression of their finished biological function, and it is a matter for rejoicing that they should be relieved of such lugubrious rituals. On the other hand, the apparent unpreparedness of many elderly hedonists for the growing debility and loss which eventually catch up with them is equally strange. When sickness and infirmity strike, the bewildered questions are increasingly heard, 'What have I done to deserve this heart attack, this stroke, this shaking of the hands, this stiffening of the limbs, these ailments, this constant ill being? Why have I become old? Why can I not do the things which I have always taken for granted? After all, my next year's holiday is booked, the house is going to be redecorated, the children are coming for Christmas. It's all arranged and paid for.'

It is one of the curiosities of contemporary culture that it frequently confuses those aspects of our lives that cannot be remedied with those that can. This is, in part, a reflection in the popular imagination of the miracles with which technology now routinely furnishes us. A news bulletin rarely finishes without some upbeat story of a cure for some hitherto incurable sickness. We have been beguiled by promises that we can escape our human destiny by the prolongation of life, by the transplant of organs, by the use of regenerative tissue. We clutch at hopes that we may escape the fate of our kind, all who have gone before. Old age can be kept at bay. We can all bathe in the waters that bestow eternal life. The intensity of living is such that we can know transcendence: mind-altering substances are available, many of them on prescription, to make us sleep or dream or escape. At the same time, there has developed a strange fatalism around things that are so obviously alterable – injustice and poverty – for instance, saying that there have always been rich and poor people and nothing you do is going to change that. It may strike future historians as odd that we seem to have confused what is existentially irremediable with what is socially contingent; that we feel more confident in our ability to rise above the limitations of our human being – among them, ageing – than to alter the immutable realities of the social arrangements.

This leads to some strange responses. To be taken by surprise by ageing, as though it were a conspiracy against us, is scarcely a more helpful response than a morbid anticipation of it, overshadowing years that might otherwise have been vigorously and usefully occupied.

We have, within the living memory of our own society, two quite contrary and irreconcilable attitudes to ageing. My mother and her sisters – born in the late nineteenth and early twentieth century – were imbued with a powerful sense of the brevity of life. They had good cause: they had seen two siblings die, and life expectancy was still only in the 40s. They were extremely morbid, they dwelt on the transitory nature of our existence and constantly repeated their conviction that justice would be done, if not in this world, certainly in the next. They met old age and decay more than halfway and liked nothing better than to sit in the churchyard on their way back from shopping, reading the epitaphs, which they knew by heart, critically appraising the message in Gothic script engraved upon the tombstones, deploring the banality of 'Asleep in God's beautiful garden', and wondering at the mystery of whether a relict was the same thing as a relic. At the same time, they expressed a kind of existential wisdom about life, highly moral, intensely puritanical. They used words like 'sorrow', 'grief', 'joy' and 'suffering' when talking about the lives of those around them, which lent a certain epic dignity to their view of existence. But they were victims of a kind of cultural melancholia, in which old age was seen as a refuge from – who knows? – unfulfilled sexuality, self-sacrifice, the slavish attendance they danced on fathers, husbands, brothers.

Life after death was a serious preoccupation for them. 'Where do they put you all?' they wondered, speaking as though the housing of the dead must be a bureaucratic nightmare. They pictured themselves reunited with those who had preceded them into death. 'It can't be so terrible if nobody ever comes back.' Sometimes they wondered if white raiment and the mansions of the blest, in the images they had retained from childhood, really existed. In a more utilitarian frame of mind, they wondered what you do all day in heaven: since their life on earth had been occupied to the last minute, they found the prospect of an eternity of leisure a little unnerving. They lived vicariously their own future absence – 'You'll know,' they said to ungrateful men, 'when you haven't got me, when I'm in my grave.' The irony was, they lived on into their 80s and 90s; and as they became very old, their obsession with death deserted them, and they became reconciled to the pleasures of a late life, enjoying the outings, the holidays, the visits to the countryside, in a way they had been unable to do in their 50s and 60s. They passed through a strange transition: during their long lifetime, they forfeited faith in the life to come without ever really gaining confidence in the here and now.

All this was swept away by the decay of an old industrial culture of poverty, and its replacement by a consumer society, in which efforts to keep at bay the evidence of ageing have become big business. The lengthening of life – especially when that life remains active and healthy – leads to an understandable desire to prolong familiar experiences. The power of habit over a long lifetime cannot be overestimated, the momentum of living creates its own power over us. One woman in her late 60s said:

> Nobody wants to admit to being old. You go to the hairdresser's, the beauty parlour, the cosmetic surgeon. I feel younger when I've had my hair done, when I've had a manicure or been to the chiropodist. You use any kind of help to avoid what you know – that you're getting old. As a woman, becoming old, you are doubly disadvantaged. People look at women for their youth and beauty – who wouldn't want to hang to both as long as she can? When you see people filtering you out of the landscape, it can make you very angry. You want to cry out to them, 'I am still here. Here I am. This is still me.' At home, I have pictures of me that prove how charming, how attractive, how *young* I was. But nobody believes me.

Western society has oscillated from one extreme to another: all the strengths and weaknesses associated with stoicism, endurance and repression have given way to the advantages and drawbacks of individualism, hedonism and self-expression. The only surprising thing is that we view ourselves as a model of balance. Industrial society has been wildly inconsistent, at one moment punitive, and at another protective of old age. Human societies rarely achieve balance. They are concerned, like any other living, natural organism, with survival.

We have passed from a time when an often exaggerated respect was extended to those who lived long to one in which the old have been comprehensively devalued. It is difficult to make sense of these changes without either falling into a hopeless nostalgia, regretting the passing of a golden age, or embracing a shallow progressivism, as though we only emerged from the dark ages the day before yesterday.

Of course, some people manage change very competently, and particularly if they are economically secure, they welcome it. It is always easier to accept new values if these are accompanied by material improvement, and any losses incurred are more likely to be passed over in silence. If these appear, they will, in any case, be felt only much later. The economic advances which have characterised Western societies in the past two generations have widened the horizons of many elderly people, in ways they would never have dreamed possible in their youth. Workers in industrial occupations expected to spend a lifetime in factory or office, in mine or mill, and then to enjoy only a limited period of straitened retirement. Increased life expectancy and generous pensions have allowed millions of elderly people to seek satisfactions denied them when they were in the prime of life.

> I went to Australia to see my son. He emigrated from Manchester nearly 20 years ago. He thought he'd make a better life there. He didn't get on very well with his father, and I think he wanted to put as much distance as he could between the two of them. He went over there for a holiday, found a job, bought a house. All in six weeks. He came home and said, 'I'm going.' The night before he left, I couldn't sleep. I went into his room when he was sleeping and kissed him, and he didn't wake up. I thought, I shall never see you again. For me, that was a moment of despair. I remembered hearing about people who went to Canada or America during the Depression; they never came home again. They sent letters and cards, but that was it. I thought it would be the same when Graham went. But after a few years he came back, and as he got on – he was in real estate – he came home more often. Then after his father died, he said to me, 'Why don't you come?' 'I'm eighty. I can't go

> there.' He came to fetch me. Oh, I shall never forget, the sight of the clouds, the mountains beneath us, the spring flowers in Adelaide. I didn't know such beauty existed in the world. It was wonderful. I wept for the joy of it; and I felt, why had we lived all our life in such cramped lives? We didn't know the world existed outside of work, the house, the pub, the shops, the pantomime at Christmas and a week's holiday in Blackpool. When we went, we took our own food for the week. We wrote our names on the eggs in indelible pencil so we wouldn't get anybody else's stale goods. It seems pathetic now. How limited we were. Of course, times change. I feel lucky I've lived to experience how wide, yet how small the world is. How beautiful, and how easy it is to go from one side of the earth to the other. I'm not religious, but I believe. I give thanks for each day, and I am happy I've been spared to see the wonderful things that have happened to me.

'I had two lives' is a familiar observation of many older people. Gavin became one of the gilded nomads of the world, passing freely between the places where they have their roots, and destinations of choice; travellers of privilege to whom no frontiers are closed. Born in 1934, the youngest of twelve children in a pit village in Fife, a small, closed community of frugal neighbourliness and conformist vigilance. Gavin always knew that he was gay, although the word was unknown at that time.

> Among the women who used to come and sit in my mother's kitchen, there was always one man. This intrigued me because I was familiar with the gender apartheid in our culture. I asked my mother, 'Why is he the only man who comes? Why doesn't he go with the men?' She said, 'Oh, he prefers it. He's different.' Difference was tolerated, as long as it was not named.

Whenever Gavin goes back to Fife now, he meets friends he was at school with – all women. They agree that Gavin and the one lesbian in the group have had a better life than they have (although the lesbian had to go through a brutal marriage before she could acknowledge her sexual preference and live with another woman). One is widowed, one divorced, one separated. They tell him they have never known the meaning of the word freedom.

Gavin left school at 15. His father, aware at the time that the mines in the area were finished, said he didn't want his sons to go down the pit. Gavin went to London at 16, and got a job in the bar at the BBC. Soon after, he emigrated to the US.

England then was very drab and hopeless. People thought the country was finished. We grew up with the memory of so many people who had emigrated in despair from Scotland – in the early twentieth century, after the First World War, during the Depression. It was hard to see Britain as a place of hope.

Everybody in Scotland had relatives in North America. Our uncles in Massachusetts sponsored me. I didn't stay with them, but went directly to San Francisco, where I did bar work. I loved it. Then came the 1960s and 1970s, the hippies and gay liberation.

One night by chance I was talking to a guy in the bar who ran a carnival that moved around California. It was not some rinky-dink outfit, but a big show, exciting rides and side-shows. He wanted someone to look after the candy wagons – spun sugar, toffee apples, sticks of candy. I said I'd give it a try. I did it for 27 years, then managed the food outlets with the show. We'd do so many days in Diego, then move on to LA, all over the state. The season lasted five months. The work was hard, but I earned enough to do what I wanted the rest of the year.

I travelled everywhere. I had a house in Manila for five years, returning to California for the season. Then I discovered Thailand. Not Bangkok, but Korat, which is the second city. I rent a town house there. I have my movies and my music. I still go to California to help with the carnival, earn a bit of extra money.

My rent in Thailand is 150 dollars a month. There are no tourists. I know everyone in the street where I live, and they know me. I can get all the young guys I want. There is a new shopping mall, as fine as anything in the US, a new swimming pool, where I go every day. I know a few *farangs*, but my neighbours are all Thai, very tolerant. I have found a community there that reminds me of Fife, but without all the secrets, without the shame. When I was a kid, there was a real feeling that our lives were not personal property, but something shared: if anyone was ill, the kids were taken in by other families. No one was abandoned. No one was left to want. That is all long gone in Fife, but I have found something similar in Thailand.

I never had a partner. I've always been promiscuous. Never get involved – keep that for friends. I see many *farangs*, they fall in love and think they've found happiness; then they find there's a whole extended family to look after. The boys like to be with their friends, they don't want to sit with old *farangs*. It's a money transaction. If you don't kid yourself it's anything else, you won't get hurt – that's the secret of survival in Thailand.

When I think of my life, I'm lucky. I'm still fit. All but one of my brothers and sisters are dead; and they died in the order they were born. I live well. I go to California once a year, Scotland once a year.

Scotland is not the same place now. It isn't the same world. I feel I've had two lives – growing up and growing older. I can't believe it. I've no one to leave my money to – anything left I'll leave to the orphanage in Korat. I'd like to give something back to the country that has given me so much and that reminds me of the community of my youth, but without the hang-ups, without the repression. I think I've had the best of both worlds.

AGEING IN POOR SOCIETIES

An old man lived with his son, daughter-in-law and grandson. The son and his wife considered him a burden and didn't want an old, physically handicapped person in their home. They decided to get rid of the problem. The son took his handicapped father in a basket and set out for the jungle, planning to leave the old man there. The grandson, observing his father's actions, said, 'Father, be sure to bring back the basket.' 'Why?' asked the father. 'Because I will need it when you grow old.' The parents reconsidered their decision. (Folk story from Bangladesh)

In an industrial town in the North of England, an old man had become a burden on his family. Unable to support him, his son decided to take him to the workhouse. The old man was unable to walk, so the son carried him on his back. As they

> climbed the hill to the workhouse, the son paused, sitting on a wall to take breath. The father said, 'Why, this is the very spot where I rested when I took my father to the workhouse 40 years ago.' The son turned back and took his father home. (Industrial folklore, oral history, 1969)

If such stories occur, in one form or another, in all cultures, this is because occasionally the similarities in our human destiny overcome chance – and basically superficial – cultural, social, ethnic or religious differences. It is significant that, in one example, the son is the teacher of the adult, and in the other, it is the father. These moral tales carry messages to the young about the proper behaviour towards elders. They transmit values which belong to societies where continuity is more important than change and in which living to be aged is a comparative rarity.

In today's world, every month 1 million people turn 60. In 2001, one in ten of the world's population was 60 or over. By 2050, this will be one in five, by 2150, possibly one in three. The fastest growth will be in developing countries, which are already home to 58 per cent of the world's elderly. This proportion is expected to rise to 70 per cent within ten years. The majority of older persons are women – 55 per cent. Women make up 65 per cent of the over-80s. Although the projected figures may be challenged, the trend is clear. In the second half of the twentieth century, 20 years were added to the average lifespan, raising global life expectancy to 66 years. This, of course, covers great differences from country to country. While Japanese women may expect to reach 80, in parts of East Africa the impact of AIDS has reduced the expectation of life to below 50.

Until recently, the preoccupation of international agencies has been, overwhelmingly, with children – children in poverty, children traumatised by conflict and war, and often compelled to fight as soldiers, children trafficked into prostitution, enslaved and bonded as labour. Above all, the fertility of the poor has been a major object of concern, and one of the main purposes of intervention has been to limit population growth.

Now the focus is shifting from 'too many children' to 'an excess' of old people. The only constant is that people – poor people – are the problem. It seems, however, that despite the United Nations Assembly on Ageing, and the declarations and plans of action, little will be done until yet another 'crisis' takes the world 'by surprise', even though it has all been long predicted. The response to the ageing of the people by governments mirrors that of individuals – they don't believe it until it actually happens.

The elderly are not, of course, a homogeneous group. A recent HelpAge Ghana survey revealed that, in the indigenous languages, there are separate terms for the 'recently old', the 'older person' and the 'very old person'. These categories are based upon the perceived capacity for work; severely practical, they nevertheless also recognise the natural *process* of ageing.

The ageing – or, to look at it more positively, the survival – of more of the world's population illustrates both the positive and negative consequences of development and global integration. Enhanced health care, especially the increasing worldwide availability of medicines and drugs, helps to keep people alive. The social and economic consequences of this, however, often disrupt patterns of care, commitment and belonging. The technical capacity to prolong life is often at odds with an apparent powerlessness to deal with the social and moral effects of this achievement.

The migrations and uprootings of people all over the world, within countries and between countries, leads to radical separations of blood and kin. In the North of Thailand, where many able-bodied people have left for the cities – primarily Bangkok – whole villages consist of only the old and children, who are dependent upon remittances. The diaspora of people from Kerala in Southern India maintains many ageing parents in old-age homes. East and Southern Africa have been the site of reverse migrations of despair, as the generation which went to the cities in search of livelihood return with only the AIDS virus to die in their home villages, while grandparents become the primary carers of their own dead children's orphans; many of these are also HIV-positive.

The majority of elderly people in the South live in rural areas, many of which have been depleted by migration: from some poor villages a large proportion of those capable of finding work elsewhere have gone. In the past, a sparse scattering of surviving elders might have been sustained by relatives and neighbours, but the numbers left behind now impose too great a burden on the able-bodied. More and more of the elderly who can no longer work depend upon money remitted home: there are whole communities in Bangladesh waiting for the monthly cash from Saudi Arabia or the United Arab Emirates. Even with only one member in a regular job in the Gulf, the livelihood of an extended family may be secured, as well as the care of those too old to work. These arrangements are extremely fragile – a broken contract, an accident at work, sheer homesickness, sudden dismissal, any of these can destroy the security of scores of people.

Indeed, many migrant workers are both exploited and unhappy. They sacrifice themselves for the sake of their family, both children and elderly parents, giving no hint to them of the humiliations, the boredom, the fatigue, the lack of privacy in barracks, servants' quarters and hostels. Behind the gangs of construction workers in the livery of some international building company sitting nervously in international airports, the smudged faces of domestic servants in virtual slavery glimpsed in the marble fortresses of Jeddah and Doha, or behind the ornamental security grilles of Knightsbridge or the Parc Monceau, the deferential drivers in the smooth limousines on the streets of global capital cities, lie stories of dispossession and hope, the anxious dependants, wives and children who do not know when they will see the familiar face again, parents convinced that the tearful leave-taking was final. Globalisation has created great opportunities for mobility, but it has also set up a war of attrition against older collectivities of family, clan, tribe or neighbourhood. Sometimes, even the old must uproot themselves and go off in search of subsistence.

> Amina Khatoon does not know her age, but she appears to be in her late 60s. Very thin, her countrywoman's eyes glazed, perhaps by the indignity of her position, she begs in Ramna Park in the Bangladeshi capital, Dhaka. She makes about 30 taka a day (60 US cents). She comes from Mymensingh, about 140 kilometres north, and her two married sons are landless labourers. Their work is seasonal. She lives with each in turn, but her contribution to her keep is her 'labour' as migrant beggar. She spends about 20 days in Dhaka, sleeping in the *mazar* (precinct) of the mosque near the High Court. There she finds food and shelter. When she has accumulated 300–400

taka, which she folds into her saree, she takes the bus home. After a few days' rest, she returns to Dhaka to begin the cycle all over again.

This is not how the family system is supposed to work. But in a society where only the strength of their bodies lies between them and utter destitution, Amina Khatoon is not seen primarily as a source of help to the family (although she may be that also, supervising the children, and performing household tasks), but as a drain on their meagre provisions. The interdependence of family remains, but each must contribute to the family income to the limits of her capacity. It has nothing to do with hard-heartedness – the hard-heartedness is entirely systemic. I met Amina Khatoon many times over a long period in the park. She feels it is her duty to ensure the survival of the family. 'I have had my life,' she says, 'I have brought up my children.' She speaks of herself in the past, as though she had died already. For her, the family is more important than the individuals in it. She feels that living to be old is not a blessing, but she does not blame her sons for sending her to beg. It is in the order of things.

Most poor families whose elders survive do everything in their power to maintain them when their health fails. This is far easier when there is a small margin of surplus out of which they can be cared for. In any case, the elderly do not become dependent until even the smallest tasks are beyond them. They continue household duties, particularly where there are small children; but caring for them is not productive labour. This should come as no real surprise to people in the West. In 1881, for instance, 73 per cent of men in Britain over the age of 65 were still working, a proportion that had fallen to about 8 per cent a century later.

Sabetun Bibi lives in a slum in the Mirpur area of Dhaka. She is about 75, and lives with her son and his family in a hut of *chetai* (woven bamboo). She came to Dhaka 50 years ago with her husband, a construction worker. He worked until the day he died ten years ago. Sabetun Bibi's seven children were all born here; among them are a fisherman, a driver, a railway worker; one has a small shop. She shares the family's food and looks after the grandchildren. She has the serene face of a woman confident that she is cared for, and who still has a valuable

> social function. It would not occur to her – or to any of her children – to think of her as dispensable or as an encumbrance.

While it is still true that the major source of care for the elderly remains with the family, the institution itself is under great strain in the context of global economic integration. It is certainly not immune to the effects of rapid economic change. As more and more people leave the home place to seek a living elsewhere, as traditional communities disperse, and the long procession of humanity moves from village to town, from rural life to the city, from the provinces to the metropolis, the bonds of kinship are stretched. But few governments can afford to put in place even the most rudimentary state provision.

And the family does, indeed, for the great majority perform the function for which it is properly celebrated. In India, I know a number of people who have sacrificed lucrative careers in the US to go back home to care for their parents, although more will go to join their young when these are abroad or if they have settled in urban areas. Relatively large families provide the chance to spread responsibility for elders among a number of people, so that the old person is absorbed into a wide network and is denied neither companionship nor a constant, though unobtrusive, supervisory watchfulness.

Globalisation places great stress on traditional societies. The South is the site of a great, untried experiment, the consequences of which are yet to appear. The International Labour Office (ILO) states:

> The extended family, the traditional mainstay of income security for the majority of people in the developing world, is becoming smaller and more dispersed. In major developing countries, about 20 per cent or more of families are headed by a woman, with no spouse present.[13]

The ILO is optimistic about the growth of an older population in the South. The report says:

> Attention is invariably focused on the increases that this will bring in the old-age dependency ratio. What is less commonly realized is that total dependency ratios will fall in the coming decades in the developing world, and fall quite steeply in the least developed countries. This is an invaluable opportunity to

> establish universal primary education for the much smaller cohorts of children reaching school age and to improve greatly the quality of the education provided – which is the best hope of achieving income security in these countries.

This reading of the position of developing countries is problematic. It is true that, even with a growing elderly population and decreasing numbers of children, there will be more people of working age. But there are few signs that these will be employed at more than survival wage rates or in the informal sector: in India, the formal sector has actually declined in the past decade and, under the influence of structural adjustment programmes imposed by international financial institutions, will decline even further. In any case, there are in South Asia tens of millions of unemployed or underemployed graduates. Many of these want nothing more than to go abroad to work in menial jobs in the Gulf, the US or Australia. Governments, under pressure to cut public expenditure, will not necessarily be in a position to increase educational provision, given all the other demands upon them, not least from those elderly no longer supported by their families. What is more, the evidence that a highly educated workforce automatically leads to 'development' is slender: economic necessity has little regard for the levels of educational attainment, and the work available does not adapt itself to their superior educational status: graduates in India are competing with each other to work in call centres. The declining number of children is, in any case, linked to further fragmenting of the family, so that the nuclear family group increasingly replaces its extended predecessor. This undermines further the capacity of people to look after parents and grandparents surviving into a later old age.

In 1998, Zeng Yi from Beijing University's Institute of Population Research[14] spoke of the importance of setting up an old age insurance scheme in China which has more than one-fifth of the world's population. This example would inspire other countries facing rapid population ageing. He said there were six main features of ageing in China: the speed of ageing; the large number of the elderly; the rapid increase of the 'oldest old' in the twenty-first century; ageing being a more serious problem in the villages; and the coexistence of rapid population growth and low per capita gross national product.

In China, people aged 65 or over will make up one-quarter of the population by 2050. China will, in a few decades, pass through changes which Europe underwent in one or two centuries. The number of older persons could reach 232–331 million between 2030 and 2050. In 1990 there were 8 million 'oldest old', that is, over 80; their number could increase to 60–160 million between 2030 and 2050.

Most governments, including that of China, are unlikely to be capable of providing social security on the scale required, as the supportive networks of kinship are extended, often to the limit. Non-governmental organisations intervene and may provide models of social care, although they cannot possibly meet more than a fraction of need. HelpAge International is perhaps the best known agency working in the field, and the contribution of charitable and religious trusts is significant. In the slums of Khartoum, the Sudanese Red Crescent not only offers care to the elderly, but has also inaugurated a programme of micro-credit for older people to set up small businesses so that they can earn, thereby not only helping them to survive, but also renewing their self-confidence and restoring their status in the community. The extension of micro-credit to the elderly is now a widely advocated method of maintaining their ability to earn.

There are three major providers of security for the elderly in the South: their own labour, the extended family and the state. The last is confined principally to the military and to government servants, who are usually covered by not ungenerous pension schemes. (This is a major reason why work in the bureaucracies is usually regarded as one of the safest jobs.) It is not surprising that we should now be hearing more about prolonging the earning capacity of the elderly. Parallels can be discerned between policies to keep people at work in the poor countries, and efforts to reintegrate the elderly into the economy in the rich world.

Just what this means for ageing people in the present is reflected in the testimony of those compelled to go on working beyond their capacities.

> Siadurahman is a cycle-rickshaw driver in Dhaka. He fought in the Liberation War of 1971, when the then East Pakistan became the independent country of Bangladesh. In the fighting he was seriously injured and lost a leg. After Independence, he lived in a shelter provided by the government for the freedom fighters. When the military came to power in 1976, he was evicted. 'With one leg and no money, what could I do?' The cycle-rickshaw is the employment of last resort for the landless and desperate. He rents the vehicle daily from the owner and earns about 75 taka a day (US $1.50). Now in his late 50s, he has a heart condition, and his one good leg has lost much of its power. He says, 'What choice do I have? I shall work until I no longer can. After that, Inshallah, I shall die.'

This is an extreme example – a consequence of a society in which there is little public provision, either for the elderly or for the 12 million disabled people in Bangladesh. Most efforts focused on retaining the elderly at work do not impose such burdens on them; but it is difficult to maintain dignity and independence through labour, particularly when people's horizons have been bounded by labour since early childhood.

In Kolkata, I met Dr Indrani Chakravarty, director of the Kolkata Metropolitan Institute of Gerontology, perhaps the most comprehensive and innovative organisation of its kind in India. From studies and surveys of the elderly to providing services for some of the poorest of the poor elderly in Kolkata, its activities are far-reaching. There are around 300,000 people over 60 in Kolkata, and about 75,000 of these live in slum areas. This relatively low proportion of elderly slum-dwellers is a reflection of the higher life expectancy of the better-off. By the age of 60, a majority of the poor will already have died.

The poor do not retire. They must continue to earn a livelihood to survive. When they become dependent, their families see them as another mouth to feed. To enhance their self-respect, the Institute runs a small employment programme in its centre in Beliaghata Road in central Kolkata. The recent banning of plastic bags by the government of West Bengal has led to a demand by shopkeepers for paper bags. This is a niche which the elderly can well supply.

About 40 elderly women and men meet each day, working from noon until two o'clock. Then they have lunch, watch TV, chat, and if they feel like it, work a little longer. The bags are made from old newspapers. Each worker earns 4 or 5 rupees a day (10 cents), a small sum, but enough to make a difference between feeling they are a charge upon their families and gaining a measure of self-reliance, making a contribution to family income.

In age, they range from early 60s to late 70s. Most are conspicuously thin: years of malnourishment, worn away, almost concave, diminutive figures of lifelong servitude. Many have harrowing stories to tell of grief, suffering and loss; but coming together for a few hours each day and realising that they are capable of doing something useful has transformed their lives.

> Bani Mukherjee was married at eleven. Her husband worked as a conductor for the Calcutta Tramway Company. He did not treat her with respect. He left his job before retirement and lost his chance of getting a pension. When he died, she was left with four sons and six daughters to care for. All have now grown up and left home. She is alone. She is given a place to sleep in the house of a neighbour, for which she pays no rent. She says the struggles of women make them stronger than men, and this is why they live longer. After her husband's death, she became a maidservant and kept the family together by working long hours in other people's houses.

> Sukhdeb Das is 76. He wears a thin dhoti and yellow shawl. Formerly a painter and decorator, he was forced to stop work 15 years ago because of failing eyesight. His wife died, his children married and moved away. They come to see him sometimes, but being day labourers and having children of their own, he understands they have nothing to give him. He lives with the wife of his eldest son, who deserted her. After the son left, Sukhdeb remained with his daughter-in-law and her two children in their rented room. She works as a maid in four or five houses each day, earning about 1,500 rupees a month (US $30). Sukhdeb was born in Diamond Harbour, 70 miles from Kolkata. He remembers the Bengal famine of 1943, when people ate *bajra* instead of rice and drank the water in which rice had been boiled, the thinnest *pantha*. Since

Sukhdeb has been able to earn a little money each day, he feels more independent. He has *friends* – a sense of being supported, knowing he is not alone, and that there are many others who share the same experience. One of the sad things about living to be old, he says, is the loneliness of surviving when all others of the same age have gone.

Radha Das is a tiny woman, probably in her early 70s. She wears a white saree and thick blue cardigan. Her face is small, there is no flesh on her arms. She lives with her two daughters. Before she came here, they were constantly quarrelling with her. One is a widow, the other works as a maid. Since Radha Das has been coming here, she is fed, gets medicine, clothing and blankets, as well as a few rupees from bag-making. Her daughters do not scold her now. She was herself a maidservant until four years ago, but she no longer has the strength to do the washing and clean the vessels. At that time, she was earning 150–200 rupees a month (US $3–4.) Her husband was a daily labourer in Uluberia, a rural area, about 40 miles from Kolkata. Radha Das was born in the city, but moved to Uluberia at the time of her marriage. There, she also worked in the fields. That was '*riot ke age*' before the riots, which is the way people refer to the time of Partition. After the death of her husband, she returned to the city and her daughters' home.

Dr Chakravarty points out one of the great differences in ageing between the middle class and the poor. 'Most people in professional life have no preparation for retirement. One day, they are working, the next they are finished. It hits them sometimes with great violence. We also work with such people. We have a supporter who gives tuition in information technology to retired people. A small group are studying here. This helps them to maintain self-respect, because they feel their loss of status less keenly.'

Dipak Mitra is a voluntary worker at the centre. He retired eleven years ago, having served in the Indian Air Force and the Department of Telecommunications. His martial air suggests discipline and control, but he speaks with great enthusiasm about 'ageing productively'. He says, 'As soon as people retire, they start to talk about themselves in the past tense: "I was

> such-and-such. I did so-and-so." It is as though they have set aside their identity. They seem to have no idea that they have a present or a future. It is for me a tonic to work with the poor. Many middle-class people have too much vanity, they cannot come down. They think it means a loss of position. They have too high a sense of their dignity, but it cramps them, and in the end strangles creativity or initiative. It is strange: we prepare for every other phase of our life, but for retirement we make no provision at all. It comes as a shock, but it shouldn't: it is an appointment we all have with time, if we live long enough. We can predict it to the day, but we thrust it from our mind and prefer not to think about it.'

Dr Chakravarty and her researchers acknowledge that respect for the elderly remains in India; whether or not this is because until recently survival into old age was a small miracle, she does not say. 'The Indian family is resilient. The *shastras* say it is the duty of an able son to look after his parents in old age. It is still a stigma here to send them to an old-age home.'

The favourable comparison which many in India make with a West allegedly grown indifferent to its elderly may be premature. It may be simply a time-lag in a culture which has not yet been so deeply penetrated by the consequences of 'development'. Dr Chakravarty recognises the tendency of the joint family to dissolve as the necessities of work take people to distant cities, to other countries.

Nor is this simply a problem of middle-class or well-to-do families. There is growing out-migration from the rural areas to towns and cities, sometimes seasonal, sometimes permanent.

In India 73 per cent of the elderly are illiterate, which means that their only option is to continue to make a livelihood through manual labour. To maintain economic productiveness is a major necessity. HelpAge India has 51 mobile medical units which can attend to some of the commonest forms of disability in the elderly. They perform 60,000 cataract operations a year – a small intervention which has a highly beneficial effect on people's power to go on working.

People are not failing to do their duty, but there is a detectable diminution of the homage traditionally paid to the elderly. In the villages, it was the custom of the young to touch the feet of elders before they began their day's duties, in order to ask for their blessings. This is in sharp decline. Within middle-class families, elders are increasingly an encumbrance. Children desire more space and resent the room occupied by elders when they have to share with brothers or sisters. One way out for the family in many poor countries is to hire servants to look after old people. There is a ready supply of cheap labour, but this is also seen as decreasingly reliable. Rarely a day passes in the metropolitan areas of India without some story of a servant who stole the property of an aged mistress, sometimes beating her, occasionally committing murder. In Delhi in 2002, I heard of an old man entrusted to the care of a servant who drugged him each day with opium, so that he could go out.

At a meeting on the International Day of the Older Person in Delhi in October 2002, the former Chief Justice of India, Dr A. S. Anand told the story of an old couple in Mumbai, who were thrown out of their own house by their two sons. The old couple pitched a tent in the garden of their home, which the daughters-in-law set fire to. Then they moved out on to the footpath. Their daughters, who were both married and living some distance away, brought meals to them, one in the morning, one in the evening. The story was published in the newspaper. A local judge took it upon himself to visit the family and to point out the inhumanity of their conduct. They begged forgiveness of the old couple, and took them back into their home. The local police 'adopted' them, and made sure that they were able to live peaceably. The judge said to the sons, 'You have no rights here. You are not tenants. You may stay here only as long as your parents give permission to do so.'

* * *

One significant outcome of the United Nations Conference on Ageing in Madrid in 2002 was the linkage of ageing with development and human rights. For the first time, this included the elderly as agents and participants in the development process. One problem with this is that the dynamic of globalisation works in quite the opposite direction, tending towards the fracturing of families, the isolation and marginalising of the elderly. The mobility of the young spirits them away from the places where lives have been rooted, anchored in community, extended or joint family, and leaves many elders marooned, often without support, or at the mercy of the charitable impulses of more distant relatives or neighbours.

The recruitment of the young for work in distant places is now occurring on a vast scale. The airports of all major cities in Asia are crowded with young men in the uniform of some transnational entity, waiting for flights to parts of the world where their labour is required. In Kuwait, I once met a young man who had been taken from his village in the north of Bangladesh to work as a goatherd: this suggests unheard-of mobility in an international division of labour, where even rural workers may become migrants to serve in lowly positions which the local people have deserted as too demeaning or ill-paid for their consideration.

Not everyone in the South views the needs of the rich economies with the same urgency that we do.

> You bribe our best academic brains. You take our educated personnel, people who have been expensively trained by India, people we need. You take our medically qualified, our nurses. You take our information technology practitioners. Then you take graduates to work in your hotels and restaurants, people who are highly qualified are transformed into a source of cheap labour. This is another form of biopiracy: even now, you are still robbing us of what we desperately need for our own survival. There are at least two malign consequences of this. One is that families get broken, and our old people feel hurt and abandoned. Then the migrants who have gone to America and Europe feel guilty. Their guilt makes them give money to extremist organisations like the VHP, the Hindu extremists and communalists. It disrupts our country twice over. (University lecturer, 50s, Bangalore)

Chapter 2

AGEING AND DEVELOPMENT

Debates about the elderly, as indeed about any other vulnerable group – children, women, sexual minorities, people with disability, threatened ethnic and religious groups everywhere, indigenous peoples – cannot be detached from wider discussions about 'development' and its meaning. The World Assembly on Ageing in Madrid declared that the elderly should be at the centre of development, but without defining it. Perhaps it is considered too obvious to mention.

When we consider the condition of the elderly, and the way they are disproportionately represented among the disadvantaged of the earth, a central question, which many had thought laid to rest by the global triumph of industrial society, returns to haunt us. Is the creation of ever more wealth synonymous with the betterment of human lives? Is the well-being of vulnerable people really dependent upon perpetually rising income, or does the creation of wealth itself militate against social cohesion, belonging and solidarity? The cosiness of the 'one-world' commitment to poverty abatement, inclusiveness, health for all, education, sufficiency and security runs up against the actual dynamic of wealth creation.

The paradox is this: more and more wealth must be created so that the needs of this or that section of the needy population can be answered; yet in the process of creating that wealth, the world is jettisoning, junking and neglecting one of its most precious resources – in this case, the accumulated knowledge and understanding of millions of lifetimes. All over the world, older people are being thrown out of work, prematurely retired, 'thrown on the scrap heap', as they sometimes describe it, being bypassed, stranded; even though at the same time, there is universal acknowledgement of the urgent need to use those wasted resources.

THE EMPLOYMENT OF THE ELDERLY

The reinsertion of the young elderly (that is, approximately those aged between 55 and 70 plus) into the economy is a problem for the West. The pattern of recent decades has been the reverse of this, namely the exclusion and early (even premature) retirement of the elderly, no matter how capable or skilled they may be. This has been partly a result of changing work practices, to which older people have become an obstacle or embarrassment ('They can't adapt', 'They are too set in their ways', 'You can't teach an old dog new tricks' represent some rationalisations of this process). Under pressure from shifting demands upon their energies, many people have voluntarily accepted early retirement, a redundancy agreement, a contract terminated on mutually acceptable terms.

Rapid technological change is eagerly embraced by industrial society and, indeed, is widely perceived as a vehicle of (economic) salvation. Scarcely a day passes without some news item about a spectacular breakthrough in medical technology, the consequences of which will conquer precisely the ills that afflict old age: a new drug to combat Parkinson's disease, a technique for 'switching off' genes that accelerate physical decline, a miracle synthesis of new drugs that will restore memory. The headline promise is rarely immediately available: it will take 15 or 20 years to perfect and test the cure; it will not be affordable by public health systems; much more research and development are needed.

Here is another strange contradiction: the development of technology, which is disemploying millions of older people, nevertheless holds out their best hope of surviving longer. As a sort of by-product of prolonging life, old people are deprived of function. This prompts the question: people may live longer, but where will they find the reason to do so?

This is one of the great conundrums unanswered by the breathless progress of 'development'. Contrary to the rhetoric, all countries are developing countries. The state of being 'developed' does not imply an achieved and stable state. It is a continuous process. The developing countries of the West have now reached a position where many of the costs of development threaten to overwhelm social cohesion, human belonging and moral values. Older questions over the impact of technology are raised once more. The Luddites, who smashed machinery which robbed them of work early in the nineteenth century, are often quoted as characteristic of a natural conservatism which makes people averse to changes, even when these are accompanied by enhanced wealth creation. The word 'Luddite' has become an abusive word which is supposed to silence anyone who even questions, much less seeks to halt, the onward march of technology and an intensifying industrialism. Industrialism has always involved the setting aside of old skills and abilities and the acquisition of new ones; as this happens, aggregate wealth increases. Since relief from poverty has been perhaps the oldest dream of humanity, and since this has been the promise that industrial society has held out for two centuries, most critics have fallen silent with each application of new technology. Yet, perversely, poverty persists. It may mutate, change its shape, but it seems intractable.

What we are seeing now is unprecedented. Dedication to scientific and technological advance has helped produce a demographic structure which threatens to overwhelm society. The very 'progress' which is supposed to offer the emancipation of humanity from premature death is imposing unsustainable costs, monetary as well as social. No one knows how to reinsert the elderly into a global employment structure whose chief features are a need for flexibility – qualities that the elderly are supposed to possess least. Globalisation, with its rapid communications industry, information-based economic activity, industries around mobility, travel and tourism, instantaneous financial transactions, entertainment and sports give precedence to the young and fit, leaving little space for the elderly.

The HelpAge Ghana survey that found that there are different words for the three ages of the elderly is relevant to all societies; although given the uneven distribution of the labour of society, the shorter life expectancy of people in poor countries, the actual age groups that make up the three categories are not the same. They depend upon the conditions in which the people grew – whether they were well nourished as children, what burden of labour they have assumed, the vicissitudes of life – plenty or hardship, peace or war.

There is a great difference between the energies and powers of the young elderly in Western society (say 55 to 70) and the very old – those over 80. In between, there is certainly a second group, whose physical and mental condition varies greatly, some remaining highly active and integrated into society, while others are frail, sick or withdrawn. This variation in the capacities of the elderly makes generalisations difficult; but one thing can be stated with certainty. There is an enormous reservoir of energy and knowledge, of astuteness and discernment, which societies suffering of a shortage of labour and dwindling numbers of young people neglect to their own detriment and loss.

As the experience of most Western countries shows over the past generation, the rich societies could not wait to discard, not merely the active elderly, but the middle-aged ones also. One of my most vivid memories from the 1980s was a visit to a house in the West Midlands, where a man who had been made redundant from a metal factory sat, head in his hands, shoulders rounded in despair, saying, 'Well, that's me finished. I'm on the junk heap. I shall never work again.' He was 38. During the 1990s, stories also began to emerge from different sectors of society of 'burnout', the exhaustion and using up of people in their late 20s and early 30s, often in the financial and banking world. Their excessive dedication to work, or perhaps, more accurately, to money, was said to have created a kind of precocious ageing. Some of them conspicuously abandoned the City and went to renovate a guest house in Provence or breed horses in Dorset.

When technology outruns the capacity of the people to adapt, it is inevitable that older people will come to be seen as incompetents, attached to the archaic practices of yesterday, while the young, always nimble and alert, soon learn to absorb new things into their lives and effortlessly respond whatever new thing is demanded of them. Only societies which are more or less static, and which transmit unchanged the tools, customs and habits that have come down through the generations, require their young to heed the teachings of their elders; and few of these remain in the modern world. Even those that have survived are under enormous pressure to abandon their ancient ways of life and integrate themselves into the spreading global market.

In such a context, it is no surprise that the idea of apprenticeship has decayed in Western society. The young man (or woman) who learns by observation, imitation and initiation into a craft or trade, painstakingly acquiring knowledge from the more experienced, has become almost an absurd idea in the West. And it is doubtless true that such a system – often requiring five or seven years of subordination and obedience – inhibited and held back capable youngsters. They were often humiliated during the period of instruction by workmen (usually men), who exercised their power to diminish and put down their youthful underlings. Apprentices were often 'indentured', which meant they often learned very little or nothing, and sometimes even had to pay for the instruction they hoped would ultimately guarantee a good job. (This abusive system still operates in many parts of the South: child workers in metal factories, welding and repair shops in India and Bangladesh often work without wages for three or four years. They may be lodged and fed by their masters while they assimilate the skills which they hope will empower them economically in later life. A similar gratuitous apprenticeship is also served by girls working as domestic servants: they are often paid in kind, their food and lodging being considered sufficient recompense for the housekeeping skills they will later apply as wives and mothers.)

A consistent disempowering of older people, especially of men, has been the common experience during the past generation, both socially and economically.

> Roger, a university lecturer, was 53 when he was offered early retirement from a university that was eliminating its history department in favour of media studies. During discussions with the authority, he protested that he had been a successful teacher for 30 years. He was told, 'You are not here to teach, you are here to facilitate learning.'

> Helen, now in her 70s, who was a psychiatric social worker based in a school for children with special needs, says the service she provided to disturbed children and their families up to the 1980s is simply no longer available. It was eliminated by public spending cuts. 'Although those salaries were saved, the costs appear elsewhere in society – in the criminal justice system, in the health service – and the price of neglect is higher, financially and socially. The problems do not disappear simply because certain skills are dispensed with.'

> Harvey, an inspirational adult education teacher, now 60, found his non-vocational classes gradually replaced by groups of reluctant teenagers taking A levels they had failed in school. He found himself unable to cope with their disruptiveness – he had never encountered an unwillingness to learn before. He was not able to redirect his skills to the changed requirements of his class. He fell ill, was physically sick. He remained on the staff until his sixtieth birthday, doing research and preparation, but retired early.

> Norman, a general practitioner, said that the best thing about his 25 years as a doctor was that it had brought him closer to retirement. 'The amount of paperwork, the aggressiveness of patients who have become the embodiment of impatience, the expectations that have been raised that nobody ought ever to be ill and that it is my duty to cure them instantaneously, have made the job increasingly oppressive, and in my view, beyond the power of anyone to do satisfactorily.'

This deskilling of professionals was a logical next step after the mass unemployment in the manufacturing sector during the 1980s. At that time, much was written about the impaired mental health of men in particular, who had grown to expect a job for life and found themselves without occupation in their 50s. This delivered a blow to the self-esteem of many, and some never recovered. In the early 1980s, I was shown the suicide note of a man in his 50s in Lancashire, in which he apologised for taking his life, which he felt had become an encumbrance to others. It was written in a shaky hand on a scrap of paper, left on the table, the sort of note you might leave for the milkman or use as a shopping list. The *casualness* of his death was as shocking as the fact of his suicide.

The confidence of older people has been undermined. Many have been overtaken by a sense of uselessness, 'a retrospective devaluing of everything I did', as one retired skilled worker said. This does not dispose those who have retired early to seek readmission into work in any form, if they can avoid it. To leave a lifetime of work, service, skill and commitment with a sense that it has all been futile or purposeless does not predispose people to seek validation elsewhere, especially if this involves skills they do not have.

One response to the loss of large numbers of older workers has been a movement towards legislation against ageism, particularly in the United States. From 2003, this will also be introduced into the European Union. There has been some success in the US in the employment and retention of older people. This is not really so much a question of legality as of culture; and culture is notoriously difficult to change by law. Even when older people do work, there seems to be a pattern: either they are doing temporary or agency work in the profession in which they were employed full time; or they are working in low-paid, less responsible jobs, often far below their capacity; or they are working without pay, either for charitable agencies or, far more likely, for their own families – especially looking after grandchildren. The International Longevity Center[1] in the US stated in March 2001 that older people are more likely than younger people to be in certain forms of 'non-traditional' employment, particularly as contract and temporary workers. Four million over-65s are currently working in the US (that is about 12 per cent of the total over 65). Here is an irony – while older people are being dismissed on the grounds that they are unable to adapt to changing practices, Charlotte Muller, director of research at the Center, says, 'Older people are very resilient. Many of them are used to the kind of job you held for life and the kind of organisation where it's very clear who the employer is and who the employee is. You can't help but admire their ability to adapt to a changing economy.' According to this, it seems they are being employed on a casual basis for the very opposite reasons why they were being ejected from the formal economy. Of course, it may be that this is not unconnected with the fact that they can be employed far more cheaply than they could when they were working on a permanent staff, with 20 or 30 years' seniority behind them.

> Efrem, who had been a local authority administrative officer, retired at 53 after a period of mental ill health. Within a couple of years he had recovered and during the following five years he kept copies of every application form he submitted. He collected four files, each with close to 100 forms. He was called for interview five or six times. More than half of the application forms received no acknowledgement. He had two brief periods

of employment, one filling shelves in Sainsbury's, which he had to give up because he could not squat to reach the lowest shelf, and the other sorting applications at a university, which was a temporary contract. Racism was a factor in some refusals, but he felt that his age was the main reason for rejection. He sat with the growing document folders around him and sank deeper into gloom. He became deeply religious, which, he says, saved him from falling into absolute despair.

THE TESTIMONY OF INDIVIDUALS

Charlotte Clements is an exceptional individual who demonstrates the possibilities not only of employment, but of the potential social usefulness of the elderly. She recognises that some of this is due to good fortune and some is a result of temperament; but she offers an inspiring example of fortitude and commitment.

Charlotte is almost 85. She is employed by Age Concern, a UK-based charity focused on the elderly. But she is not working in a charity store. She runs Keep Fit classes for the elderly four days a week. Until recently she also gave swimming classes, but had to give it up because the chlorine in the water was damaging the skin on her feet.

> I worked in the rag trade when I left school, but when the war broke out, I became a nurse. That really made me. After the war I was offered a hospital job, but since I'd been separated from my husband by five and a half years of war, I didn't want to do nights away from him. I worked in a meat products company, and then I went to Heinz Foods, where I was a supervisor for 28 years. I loved it. At that time, companies didn't employ married women, you had to wear your wedding ring around your neck. Generally, you were expected to work till marriage, then the company would give you a dowry. I had the toughest department in Heinz, the labelling department, where all the young boys and girls worked. They were always falling in and out of love, I heard all about their lives. I adored my job. Eventually, Heinz started its own training department. I had to be able to do every job, so that I could place disabled people, difficult people, older people in the appropriate place. I later became welfare officer.

In 1952 when I started we employed 10,000 people. By the time I finished in 1978 it was down to 1,000. It was a very progressive company. I had five shillings to buy flowers and fruit for every employee who was sick for more than three weeks. We had retirement parties; I would get the local photographer along from the paper and order a cake, so they would leave on a high, feeling their work had been valued.

If a girl employee became pregnant, we had a home in Finsbury Park where she could go and have the baby and stay for six weeks, and a job was kept open for her. They believed that if they took care of the workers the workers would take care of them. Every can of food that was dented they sold to the workers for a penny. They could buy a big bag of stuff for two shillings. There was no theft. I still kept my single name through all my working life. Women were second-class citizens.

I helped get the first black people into Heinz. There was a secret ballot in the canteen; and it was agreed we would take 20. This was 1960. They were all put in the same department, making up Christmas hampers – it was the simplest task. Everybody thought they still lived in straw huts. Then I had to write a report for the company. I said there was no difference between them and us, except that they had had more sun on their faces. So they were admitted into other departments. Quite a few supervisors resigned over it.

It wasn't like going to work. My husband worked for British Road Services. This young man and a crowd of boys used to see us walking up and down the street. One day a boy came up to me and said, 'He's sweet on you.' I said, 'I wouldn't walk down the street with him.' Anyway, we married.

I adored my father. He was my guide and inspiration in life. He even used to come with me when I bought a coat. We were a happy family, six children. My mother, father, one brother and a sister were all killed one night when a bomb fell on their air-raid shelter. It was what they called an oil bomb, a kind of drum packed with oil and explosives. They suffocated in the shelter. I was away nursing. It took them nine weeks to find me, they were all buried by the time I came to know. My brother was 14; he'd just got a scholarship to go to the Bluecoats School. I felt guilty. I had been helping others, but I hadn't been able to help my own family.

My husband died after 30 years of marriage. He was heavy smoker and died of bronchial pneumonia. I had worked with my second husband at Heinz. He had lost his wife and we comforted one another. We used to go out together, dancing and so on, and I was seen in his car. He said, 'People will talk.' I said, 'I don't mind.' He said, 'I do.' So we got married in 1972. He died in 1983.

My life began again after retirement. I felt I was wasting time not working at 60. The local authority were training people in a group called Action Sport. I got trained with the elderly people at the Caribbean club, then offered my services to the Pensioners' Resource Centre. Age Concern gave a couple of rooms for advice work and Keep Fit classes. They started by giving me an honorarium, then they employed me. I've been doing Keep Fit for the elderly for 20 years. It's a kind of physiotherapy to music. So many older people have become unfit – maybe they've done sedentary jobs, they've driven in their cars, they haven't kept themselves in good condition. So we aim to make them more mobile. Many elderly only think of eating and sleeping and going to Bingo after retirement. All the people in my classes are now younger than I am. I'm a kind of Mother Superior, I fill in forms, I help them do probate for wills if they can't afford a solicitor, I advise them what is available for older people. I've never stopped learning.

I forget how old I am until somebody asks me. One day a policeman stood at the road crossing. He said to me, 'Come on, Ma.' That was about 15 years ago. That's when I knew I appeared old.

I've always wanted to help people, in the way my mother did. There was always a woman in every street who helped lay out the dead and bring babies into the world, before people had access to medical services. When someone went to hospital, a neighbour would take the children in, somebody else would give them their meals. People are not friends any more. We've stopped being human. We have such experience of life and the world, only nobody wants to know. Nobody asks. Nobody listens. They think after retirement your brain stops.

Most of my class are retired people – they are arthritic, they suffer from depression and diabetes. To them it is a lifeline. Most are black or Irish. I used to teach indoor bowling to the homeless men from the Salvation Army Hostel. I was given an award in 1997 for work in the community. We went to the Hilton Hotel and the award was given by Princess Diana. It was wonderful. She was such a charmer. She spoke to everyone, and even if her schedule was late, she would never break off until the conversation was finished. I've had a wonderful life; and meeting Princess Diana was my best moment.

Charlotte Clements is still working. She does not do so out of economic necessity, but because she has the energy, the commitment and the will to contribute to the work of society. When these arise out of an inner drive, as long as work is available, this presents no problem. But when it becomes a matter of compulsion – say, by raising the retirement age – it is likely to be resisted. It is one thing to talk about the capacities of elders in the abstract, but quite another to realise them effectively.

In any case, older people perform a great deal of unpaid labour, much of it in relation to their own families, whether it is caring for a sick spouse, or a sibling, or much more often grandchildren. This is part of an enormous uncounted labour force in the world, consisting mainly of women. Increasing numbers of elderly people also find their retirement is a time not of relaxation but of caring for their own very aged and frail parents.

My mother lived until she was 93. For the last five years of her life she was completely dependent on me. I can truthfully say that during those years I never knew what a good night's sleep was. I slept with my mind half-awake, alert, listening. The tension was terrible. I lay there in the night, listening. I imagined I heard her call out, crying, trying to get out of bed. I would wake up, my heart pounding – was that the echo of her voice, or was it the central heating? My whole life revolved around her needs. I don't regret any of it. I did my duty to her. She loved me and I did what was necessary. I had no other dependants. I never married. Since she died, even now I have nightmares – she is still here, she needs me and I cannot reach her. Sometimes I wake up crying. But generally, now, I know a peace I never had before, since I did the best I could. I have nothing to reproach myself with. That gives me great satisfaction. My mother was very religious, we went to the Wesleyan chapel. She never doubted that we would be reunited in

> heaven. I don't know about that. All I know is I did what I thought right as long as she was on earth.

When this woman's mother died, she was in her 60s, and she found the freedom she acquired both terrifying and onerous. She found occupation in the work of the local chapel, but said, 'The chapel is also an empty place. It doesn't really belong to the community any more. It is a refuge for people like me – the old, the ugly and the useless. We keep each other company, and sing the praises of a God who has left us in the lurch.'

Many women, particularly those who remained unmarried and stayed at home to nurse their elderly parents, are now regarded as having 'sacrificed' their lives. For most, there was little choice. They were often referred to as 'old maids' and looked upon with a kind of pitying respect. Such lives may now be regarded as 'wasted', but when the work of cherishing loved ones is prompted by devotion, what they have done is both dignified and essential to the wider well-being of society. We may wonder whether such selflessness will be present in a new generation. When I was a child, we lived next door to an old woman, then in her 80s, who was looked after by her son, a factory worker then in his 50s. He would say, quite unselfconsciously, 'My Mam is my only sweetheart.' He would sit by her chair in the late afternoon sun and hold her hand. She would say, 'He's better than any daughter could have been.' Today, he would probably be called gay, although he almost certainly never came to any recognition of his own sexual needs.

The most significant work of the elderly is in the care of grandchildren, particularly when these are very young.

> Ann Naylor is in her early 80s. She has lived in a residential home in the North of England for just over three years. She's a small woman, alert and attentive, but very frail as a result of osteoporosis. She moves with difficulty, using a frame, and has had a number of falls, leading to fractures and broken legs. She was widowed 20 years ago. She lived with her son, his wife and their two children until she went into residential care. She feels bitter that while the children were dependent, her son was happy to keep her at home. She says that she effectively brought up the grandchildren, because both parents were working. Their mother went back to her job as manageress in

a big retail store within weeks of her daughter's birth. 'When they were young, I did a lot of work around the house, as well as look after them. I kept them occupied, read to them, played with them. I was quite young then, still in my 60s. When they started school, I took them and waited for them outside the school gate in all weathers. I was always there when they came home. I made their meals and put them to bed. I was really an unpaid nanny. But they helped to keep me young.

'As the children became more independent, 13 or 14, they didn't need me so much. I could accept that. But I noticed that my son became more impatient with me. There was a definite cooling of the atmosphere. I know I was getting slower, and I couldn't remember things so well. That was when I had my first fall.

'My son and the grandchildren come to see me. But when I felt I needed help, I needed to be looked after, it just wasn't there. Of course, I understand they have their reasons. They both have good jobs. My daughter-in-law is quite the businesswoman, she dresses very smartly, she has authority in the store. They were very reasonable about it. They started saying, "We can't look after you, Mum. Wouldn't it be a good idea if you found somewhere?" If you found somewhere. Those were the very words. It cut me to the heart. Not even "We'll look for a place somewhere." "If you found somewhere" – almost as though it was my responsibility to take myself off their hands.

'When you grow older, you think, Oh yes, I'll look after the grandchildren. It makes you feel you are safe for life. But actually, it isn't a guarantee of care. It's a bit like a reprieve from execution. Part of me doesn't blame them – it's just the way things are. But part of me is very angry. Why have they left me here? It isn't a bad place, but there is no one here I would choose to spend my time with. Why does anybody think that being old gives you enough in common with everybody else who is old? Do they think we're going to wander hand in hand down Memory Lane for the rest of our lives? A lot of people here are selfish and stupid, and I'm not either of those. Then again, I think, Well, they really didn't have a choice. How could I expect them to give up their jobs when they need the income? They don't really have much more choice than I do. But that doesn't mean I rejoice over it.'

For most people, duty to those they love is not regarded as work, even less as 'labour'. It is part of the freely given, without which society would indeed fall apart.

> My mother and her sister had lived together since my mother was divorced and my aunt widowed. My mother and aunt went into a nursing home together when they were 83 and 90 respectively. My mother was severely disabled and could not get up or feed herself: each spent far longer together than either had with her marriage partner. My aunt, although seven years older than my mother, looked after her until she could no longer do so. My aunt had waited on her husband, invalided out of the Navy after he contracted TB: he had been on a ship during the Russian Revolution, and had taken white Russians off the Northern Coast near Novaya Zemlya. In the 1920s, when she married him, he was told he would have no more than a year to live. Her care for him prolonged his life by at least 20 years. For my aunt, it was natural that when my mother became dependent, she would look after her. She remained serene and optimistic, although my mother was 'difficult', demanding and punitive by turns.
>
> They shared a room in the nursing home. My aunt fell sick and was taken into hospital. After two or three weeks, it was decided that nothing more could be done for her, and in any case, she was 'blocking' a bed urgently needed. When she was taken back to the nursing home, my mother refused to have her in the same room. My aunt died that same night.
>
> As a child, my mother regularly entreated me, 'Promise me, whatever happens, you won't let me finish up in a home.' She spoke with passionate solemnity. Tearfully, desperately I vowed that such a thing was impossible. But by the time she became old, the family had dispersed, society had been transformed, and going into a home was both a relief and a natural next step when she and her sister could no longer manage the house they had shared for 35 years.

The dedication of carers of the elderly cannot be costed in the exhaustive and spreading calculus of the market. It is impossible to measure the accumulated 'capital' that binds the lives of people together, that ties up our existence with kin, companions or loved ones. Of course, 'care packages' that are offered to keep people in their own homes, the 'inputs' required to maintain independence, the stay in hospital, the cost of home helps or meals-on-wheels or home nursing, all have a price. But most people still receive the priceless tenderness and merciful devotion freely given by those with whom they have shared their lives.

Freda's husband was diagnosed with Alzheimer's about three years ago, although she subsequently realised he had been displaying symptoms for the two previous years.

> The first sign was that he had to give up driving, because he was doing it so badly. Then he had pancreatic problems and, while in hospital, behaved strangely. I went with him to the doctor's. The doctor asked who was the Prime Minister and all the usual questions, and then said, 'Oh, it's just memory loss.'
>
> Later, it became clear, and the doctor spelt out that it was Alzheimer's. I told Doug, he said, 'Yes.' I said, 'Let's carry on and do what we can.' We continued to go to shows, he loves the theatre. The only difference was that we went by bus. We kept on dancing, he's a good ballroom dancer. I used to teach ballet. Not now, I'm 76. We belong to the church, and he enjoys the services.
>
> It gets worse, of course. He's on Aricept, which delays the speed at which it develops but of course can't stop it. He tries to read, but can't maintain the interest to finish it. We have parties booked for Christmas, you have to carry on being positive, doing what you've always done. My neighbours have been fantastic.
>
> I hold coffee mornings, raising money for Alzheimer's; you find so many people whose lives have been touched by it in one way or another. The thing to do is not sit and brood. I found out all there is to know about Alzheimer's. I go to meetings of carers. My husband is 80 in a month's time.
>
> I had a minor stroke a few weeks ago. It shook me. You realise your limits. I don't feel old. Inside, I feel the same as when I was 20. My husband is happy. He doesn't understand why I'm not.
>
> My thought is that I might not have enough time to do all I want to do. This is my second marriage. I was widowed at 45 with two children. I had my stroke on our sixteenth anniver-

sary. We belong to a group which calls itself Young at Heart. We have 60 members, it grew out of a retirement class.

Doug goes to a day centre, not every day of the week. It costs £3.40 a day, and we couldn't afford it . When we go on holiday, you share a table with others. I always tell them straight away. Everybody is sympathetic.

He got worse when I was ill. One of Doug's symptoms is that he thinks he's travelled the world. Everything he sees, he knows the Queen, he's been knighted, and so he says he's happy to sit back now. He really believes he's done all the things he wanted to.

Patience is difficult at times. If I say, 'Oh, Doug', at some of the things he says, he says, 'Are you calling me a liar?' Normally he's happy, but this has made him aggressive. He used to work for Ford's. He was union secretary. He loved his job.

I've always kept going. My mother died when she was 80, and I used to go and cook for my father and look after his house. When I was widowed I started the local group for one-parent families, I've always been a doer.

I am frightened of getting older, because I feel there's not much time. I don't like the way people treat you – they see you as an old age pensioner, they don't see all the experience and knowledge you have inside you; above all, they don't see your intelligence and capability for living. I'll carry on as long as I can. I wouldn't dream of doing anything else.

It is one thing to speak of 'reintegrating' older workers into the labour force, but this disregards a more fundamental question: if such people are to be engaged stacking supermarket shelves, performing routine tasks in offices and banks, learning IT skills or working in retail outlets, who will do the work of tending to those afflicted by the ills to which older people are always prey – the wearing out of the body, the disturbances of the spirit, the victims of cancer, heart attack or stroke? For it is not the health services which bear the principal burden of this work, but the tireless self-abnegation of those they love. What kind of economic sense would it make to compel such people to earn the money required to pay strangers to perform the same work, only with less care and greater indifference than the people for whom they represent unique, irreplaceable husbands, wives, frail parents or even children? To seek answers to social and moral problems in the realm of economics is a strange project indeed, but it is one to which are constantly bidden.

WORKED TO DEATH

Poor people in the South do not have a choice about whether or not they will work into old age. Most simply do it, because that is the way life is and always has been. At the same time, an absence of even the most basic safety nets also compels them to look after the needs of their families, to provide them with whatever care or nursing they may require. No question of 'reintegration' here.

> Ganga Devi is in her 60s. Her father was a farmer who had become landless by the time he had married his three daughters – indeed, he sold his last remaining piece of land to pay for their dowry. Ganga Devi went to live with her husband's family close to Kanpur in North India, where two brothers owned 8 *bighas* of land (2 or 3 acres). They had two children. Five years after the marriage, Ganga Devi's husband died of tetanus. His brothers and their wives simply turned her out of the house, together with her two children, then aged four and two. She would not return to her family's house, since her father was elderly and her mother close to death. One night she took a small bundle of possessions and the children and started walking. It was the time of the monsoon, and the rain was unrelenting. She walked for three days across Uttar Pradesh. The family were fed on the road by villagers who came out to ask where she was going. Everywhere she asked if there was any work and a place which would also accommodate her children. At last, on the road to Varanasi, she was taken by a woman to a landowner with extensive holdings who was willing to take her as a domestic servant and labourer. This family offered her a single room, a dilapidated and run-down cowshed. There she and her children settled, and she began work in the ramshackle farmhouse.
>
> She worked without wages, but received basic foodstuffs, clothing and blankets. She worked all hours. She cleaned and, later, because she was of Rajput caste, cooked for her

employers. She collected fodder for the buffaloes, and did the weeding, transplanting and harvesting in the fields. Her days were defined only by her labour. She barely had time to prepare food for her children. At five, her daughter had already begun to look after the house and take care of her brother during their mother's long days in the fields. There was no question of her going to school, but as soon as her brother was old enough he was sent for education, and this made the sister 'free' to help her mother with her labour. She minded the cattle and gathered firewood for cooking.

Although the landlord gave her no money, he promised Ganga Devi he would one day give her some land of her own. It was more than ten years before he redeemed this promise; and at the same time, because of the service she had given, he granted her a small daily wage. She had made herself indispensable to the family, taking care of his mother, an elderly autocrat, as well as running the household. After she had repaired the shelter, Ganga Devi never spent a single rupee of this money. She saved it, twisted in a piece of cloth in a hole in the earthen floor. She started to grow food on the three *bighas* of land she had been given; and she lived a life of extreme frugality, taking out the precious bundle of notes and coins only when she had to buy something indispensable for her son's education.

The boy finished school and went to college, where he took a BA in commerce. He was subsidised by his mother and sister, who effaced themselves so that he might gain the advantages that would, one day, benefit them also. When he left college, there was no work other than giving tuition to other boys in the surrounding villages, so that they might follow him on the path to a rewardless education. He gave all the money he earned to his mother.

Then he found employment in a company in Varanasi which assembled and sold garments. A conscientious young man, he gave most of what he earned to his mother, who nevertheless lamented his extravagance whenever she saw him in a new shirt or pair of trousers, and declared he would eat up everything she had saved. After some years, she was able to buy a further two *bighas* of land with the money she had hoarded so carefully.

Her daughter married, but her new husband's family mistreated her. He beat her badly and broke her arm, which never healed properly. She returned to her mother's house. She worked in the house of the landlord, without wages. They saw the landlord as a benefactor since he had taken them in when they were destitute – a bottomless gratitude which tied them into dependency and exploitation.

The son got married and brought his wife into the house, which he reconstructed, with a concrete floor and tiled roof. He planted some chillies and lemon trees, and a few canna lilies around the house. He now has two children of his own.

Ganga Devi was worn out at 62. A tiny, thin woman, she had lost many teeth. She became arthritic and was barely able to walk. But she knew nothing else than going out at sunrise every morning, picking fodder for the two buffaloes they had bought. Her headload was familiar in the area, bobbing up and down through the long grass, since she walked with great difficulty as she grew older.

Defined by labour, by 40 years of servitude, work was her sole identity, as it is of her daughter who, at 37, already seems to be well into middle age. Ganga Devi could have worked less, but she did not trust anyone else to perform the tasks that had become second nature to her. She criticised her daughter-in-law, whom she accused of laziness, of not preparing food properly, of leaving stones in the rice and not scouring the vessels with grit properly so that they would shine on the blue-painted shelf in the kitchen.

Ganga Devi constantly complained to herself, a soft continuous murmur, against those who never knew the meaning of work, who did not do their duty, did not honour their parents. She could not have ceased working. The idea of 'retirement' would have been meaningless to her: only a labour abridged by death.

The little house was a modest enough place, but pretty, and covered with sweet-smelling creeper. It would be impossible to measure what went into the creation of that small, unremarkable shelter, what a lifetime of energy, anxiety, unflagging labour and will-power was absorbed by this unobtrusive structure among the whispering grasses of the plains of Uttar Pradesh.

> And Ganga Devi did die, as might have been predicted, while working. One evening when she failed to come home at dusk, she was found lying among the grass she had cut, the little hand scythe with its blade shiny and its worn wooden handle beside her. They carried her home, light as a grasshopper, said her daughter, who held her in her arms and placed her on the bedding. She died the same evening in front of the little shrine she had constructed, where she had performed puja every morning before starting the work which at last claimed her life.

That they will work until the end is the expectation of hundreds of millions of people all over the world; and to them, the fate of Ganga Devi would not be regarded as unfortunate or dishonourable. They ask nothing more than to die without becoming a burden to their children, no matter what efforts they have made to ensure the survival of the next generation.

In the last few decades, the poor elderly from the rural areas, left without any means of livelihood, have been joining their children in the city slums. They are not always welcome.

Subhashnagar is a *jhuggi-jopri* (slum) settlement in West Delhi, on the edge of the sprawling capital city, with its population of 12 million or so. It is a place of rough brick shelters, roofs of polythene or corrugated metal, weighed down by stones, rusty bicycle wheels, old baskets – anything to stop them blowing away in the gusty monsoon winds. Narrow alleys between the houses are cut by crooked channels of waste water, sluggish grey streams that gather in stagnant pools wherever there is a dip in the ground. Heaps of garbage – vegetable waste decaying beneath the claws of scavenging blue-black crows with bright yellow beaks – send out a gaseous stench that pervades the whole community. The area was settled by rural migrants in the 1960s and 1970s.

Someone brings a broken *charpai* (a string bed on a wooden frame) close to the entrance of the slum where rusty barbed wire marks the limit of the settlement. A group of elderly people wait in line, as though telling their story to a foreigner was simply another expectation arbitrarily imposed upon them; yet another of the daily accounts they must give of themselves to police, officials, bureaucrats and the grudging administrators of scant charity.

Poona is about 75. She came from Mordabad in Uttar Pradesh 15 years ago when her husband died. She has two children. She says simply, 'My son feeds me', as though this were the limit of what she can hope for in life. Until recently she was working in a flour mill, but she had to leave because breathing in the flour dust left her with a permanent cough. Her son had a small eating-stall – a few benches and rough wooden tables beside a cooker served by a gas cylinder – where he prepared food for the construction workers and cycle-rickshaw drivers who live in the slum. The police destroyed it because he could not afford to pay the 500 rupees they demanded each week. He now works as a rickshaw driver, earning between 60 and 80 rupees a day (US $1.20 to 1.50). He has four children. Poona says, 'A daughter-in-law is good only if a son is good. Who would not like to live in the village? But there is no food. In Delhi I eat one meal a day, chapatti and vegetable. Old age has no appetite.'

Ramdevi is 60. Her husband, a day labourer and rickshaw driver, died of TB ten years ago. Ramdevi had no land in her village near Lucknow, so she came to Delhi with her four daughters, two of whom are married. In spite of her own ill health, she works in two houses as a maidservant, washing vessels and cleaning floors. She also has three sons, who live separately from her. They give her nothing. Ramdevi earns between 800 and 1,000 rupees a month (US $16–18). The people she works for give her stale chapattis, but have no concern for her well-being. 'If I am sick and miss two days, they dismiss me, and I have to find work somewhere else. I will need a dowry of 30,000 rupees to marry each of my daughters. Where will I find such a sum when we live on 30 rupees a day?'

Laxmi says she is 60. Many elderly people in India say they are 60. This is a symbolic rather than a chronological age since it suggests a great age in a country where, until recently, people died young. In fact, life expectancy in India is now about 63; but among the poor survival until 60 still seems a noteworthy achievement. In any case, many poor people do not know their age. Laxmi says, 'No one listens to us because we are old. If my grandson wants to help me, his mother calls him away. I have one son who is not in his senses, and who will never marry. I work as a rag-picker, and he works with me. We go out early in the morning. I collect and sell rags for 5–6 rupees a day (about 10 US cents), and my son gets the same. We eat *roti* and vegetables once a day. All the time I am thinking, Who will take care of him when I am gone?

Maya, also in her 60s, has a son and a daughter. Her son has TB and no children. Her daughter has two children who are sickly. Maya had a second daughter who died, leaving three children. The husband abandoned them, so Maya also takes care of them: one of these, a boy, is mentally ill. Their father was, in any case, addicted to drink. He sold his *jhuggi* (hut) for 40,000 rupees (about US $800) before he disappeared. Maya is a vegetable vendor in the middle class suburbs, and earns 30–40 rupees a day (70–80 cents). Since this is an illegal settlement, they pay no rent, but there is constant insecurity, since the Delhi government is systematically demolishing the slums.

Mamata, 65, is ill: her stomach is distended, obviously, as she says, not from an excess of food. Mamata has two daughters and a son. The son is married, with four children, although he does not look after them properly – he beats and abuses them. Mamata lives with her husband, formerly a rickshaw driver, but now worn out and no longer able to work. Mamata is the only earning member of the family. She sells *saag* (spinach) and other green vegetables which she carries through the streets in a shallow basket on her head. 'I carry vegetables in the streets, but now my neck has become very weak, and I cannot carry enough to make a good living. I earn between 20 and 30 rupees a day (50 cents). My daughter is married, but she is not happy because her husband drinks. When the children come to my home, I have nothing to offer them. They are working – one in a brick kiln, the other as a maidservant. My son's children do not care for me, since they are like their father who neglects me. In any case, he is a rickshaw puller, he must feed his four children first. How can he help me? He doesn't come to visit. Nobody cares for you when you are old. This is our fate. This is our misfortune.'

'Is it better to live to be old or to die young?' I asked. Mamata said, 'If our children do not care for us, we should die by accident, or we should go on the road and be killed by a lorry, or we should take poison.' 'Why do we live to be so old?' asked Maya. 'It is because in our youth we ate village food when ghee and fresh milk were plentiful. Our children do not get these things, and that is why they are weak.'

Kasturi is 70. A small, frail woman who can scarcely see or hear, she is from Aligarh. She lives with her son, but he does not take care of her. He is a hawker who sells fruit. He has four children and earns about 1,500 rupees a month (US $30). 'It is only natural that he should feed them first. Sometimes, my grandchildren sit with me, but my son does not. My husband died four years ago. He had arthritis, but the doctor gave him the wrong medicine and he died. I came here to be with my son. I did not want to leave the village, but if there is no one to give you food, where will you go?'

Saburti, who is over 80, lost her husband 20 years ago. He fell on the building site where he was working as a construction labourer. Saburti is too old to work. She must go to the temple and ask for food, both for herself and her daughter, who, she says, is mad. There is no one else. 'Where shall we go? We can roam the roads all day, but that will not fill our bellies.' The elderly poor are small, so thin they are almost two-dimensional, with the thin sticks of their arms, their bony legs, the rib-cage visible with the heart pulsing against it.

Ram Krishna is an old man of 80. He used to carry cement on building sites, but now his joints are too weak to support him. His wife works as a domestic in rich people's houses. She, too, has arthritis. 'I have one son, but he does not work. He stays at home while his mother wears herself to death to feed him. Our children should now be looking after us, but, instead, we must provide for them. I came to Delhi because Indira Gandhi came to our village and said, 'Come to Delhi, there is work for everyone.'

Jyoti Ram is about 60. He was one of the few people in Subhashnagar who said he was reasonably content. He used to be a *bheldari* worker (builder's labourer). He is given food by his

> nephews or, more accurately, by their wives, since his wife is dead and his four children died in infancy. He sleeps outside on a *charpai*. In the rain, he has a plastic cover. 'If they feed me, what more can I expect? Old age is sorrow. I left work five years ago. My nephews give me clothes and some *bidis* (cheap cigarettes). No one cares for the old. No one asks our advice. You get food – this is the limit of the respect you can ask for. People in the villages have warmer hearts but no money. You cannot eat kindness, but food given grudgingly is also bitter.'

From these brief insights into the fate of the elderly poor, certain experiences recur that are repeated all over Asia and Africa. Firstly, the thinness of the fabric of family protection and belonging: although in some cases it has broken down completely, the majority still fulfil their duty, however sparingly. Secondly, people have learned to make only the most modest demands: one old woman said the only thing she dreams of is food. Thirdly, the pressure to go on working is relentless, even when their bodies are used up by work. Fourthly, many older people must uproot themselves late in life to follow their children to the cities. Fifthly, it is clear how widespread are disability, mental breakdown and disorder, burdens which parents, especially mothers, have to bear into old age. None of these things is unique to India. Indeed, in less aggravated form, they haunt the imagination of older people everywhere. They are much mitigated in the rich world; but with the menace of declining security for future generations, we may see closer convergence between the West and the South in the years to come.

FALLING LIFE EXPECTANCY IN AFRICA

Just as the need to continue work (either paid or self-provisioning) into old age is more desperate in the South, so, too, is the urgency of caring for the sick and the abandoned of all ages. If the quiet stoicism of elderly women in the West is heroic, how much more so is the endurance of those who care for dependants without resources, with a negligible income. In East and Southern Africa, where 80 per cent of the confirmed cases of AIDS in the world are concentrated, the last two decades have created a new phenomenon: a generation of active young people wiped out, while their children have been, in a reversal of inheritance, left to the very grandparents whose expectation was that they would be the ones cared for in old age.

Elise Mahagendu works with a non-governmental organisation in Tanzania, devoted to AIDS orphans and their carers. Her own husband died of AIDS and she is herself HIV-positive. She was forced by prejudice to leave her job in a government ministry. She had no other means of livelihood, and her children were still at school. In despair, she went for counselling. There, she discovered that she had a talent for helping others. She says,

> I am not afraid to speak out. My family didn't like it at first, but they have come to see the value of honesty and the folly of silence. Poverty makes people more vulnerable to HIV, and then HIV increases their poverty. A majority of orphans are with their grandparents, many of whom are over 60 and never learned to read or write. They have no resources to care for the children. They themselves were depending on the parents of these orphans. They are often without land, without shelter, without food.
>
> In one village, two orphans lived with their grandmother in a one-room hut. When it rains, the floor is flooded. One died of pneumonia. HIV-positive children are liable to infections, TB, skin diseases, lung infections. My husband's parents are still alive and in their 70s. Since he was the only son, they expected everything from him. They were traumatised by his death. His mother became seriously disturbed, a psychiatric patient, because she was convinced that her son was not really dead and would come back. Everything goes against nature. This was ten years ago. At that time, there were many people to comfort her and bring her back into her right mind. Since then, so many have died that the support is no longer there. People are left to go mad with grief and solitude.
>
> The stigma and shame remain, because it is not in our culture to talk about sex. The shame passes to all the people around the one who suffers. When someone dies, to save face people claim that the cause of death is something else. Even the grandparents who look after the children may not be respected. They are often rejected and discriminated against. The stigma about HIV is slowly being reduced, but in rural

areas, people still do not know the mode of transmission. They think that you can get it by shaking hands or using the same glass. They would throw everything away that has been used by the patient.

It is a big burden on old people. The basic needs of the elderly were taken care of by their children, and then suddenly it stops. The money doesn't come. But the children return home to die. You have to fall back on what you have at the time when you are least able, when you have no strength and no money. If your son is sick for a whole year before dying, resources are exhausted. But for most, after the diagnosis, time is short. Those who can access drugs or good nutrition live longer, but in the poor villages, the death sentence is not commuted.

Some households where the grandparents have died are now headed by children. The elders make great sacrifices, but they have neither the knowledge nor the means. Many people say, 'Oh, the African family is close-knit, they provide social security.' But how can people whose powers are failing look after children? If the children are healthy, they may be too boisterous and energetic. If they are sick, how can the old tend them and give them the nursing they need? The wisdom of the old people runs out. The support is falling away. A whole culture is being obliterated. Old people see their children bringing home, not wealth from the city, but a coffin in which their body lies.

Life expectancy in our country was 53. Now it is 46.

As AIDS has swept through Africa, it is not governments and their stretched health service, not international donors, certainly not the financial institutions, and even less the pharmaceutical companies that have held society together; it is the uncelebrated kindliness and humanity of millions of ordinary people, most of them older women, who do not need to be taught the urgency of keeping hope alive for the abandoned and orphaned. They just do it.

It is estimated that about 40 million people worldwide are affected. No one knows exactly how many people in Tanzania are HIV-positive. It is admitted that official statistics probably record no more than one-fifth of the cases.

Few places remain untouched. 'Whenever you go home,' people say, 'you do not ask after the missing. You know their fate.' Some families have lost a whole generation: one woman buried all her seven children. The people who went to the city come back with nothing, 'not even the flesh on their bones'.

The old must resign themselves to seeing their children predecease them, and the world is turned upside down. They must find the strength to take care of their dead children's children. A new generation wastes away, while the elders live on, incapable of providing even the nourishment that will prolong, even for a few months, the lives of those entrusted to their care. No wonder millenarian Christian sects flourish and Islamic fundamentalism gains ground – what else will reconcile people to this denatured world? Outside the Lutheran church in Dar es Salaam, a cassette player on a rough handcart plays religious songs: Elvis recites the Lord's Prayer, sings 'You'll Never Walk Alone'.

Asha Likele lives in Luis Mbeza, just outside Dar es Salaam. The community was created by the villagisation programme of Julius Nyerere in the 1970s. Asha had to move only a few kilometres from her hillside *shamba*, which she continued to cultivate in the time left free from her duties on the communal land.

Now in her early 60s, she is looking after six children orphaned by AIDS – four boys and two girls aged between five and sixteen. These represent six dead parents. Originally, her elder brother had taken some of them into his home, but when he, too, died, she assumed responsibility for all six. She says,

> Allah did not bless me with children of my own. They call me Mother, since all but the oldest came to me when they were very young. Other children tell them I am not their mother, but even though they know it, they choose not to believe them.
>
> I live from farming, so the income is small. Ten acres inherited from my father is enough to feed the seven of us and to sell something in the market as well. I rent out a room in my house. One sister helps me work on the farm. Salehe, my eldest, does not want to do farm work. Young people look down on growing food. They know only money, and think the produce of the earth is worthless because there is nothing to

show for many months. They want a tender, that is, money that comes every day or every week. Salehe wants to learn mechanical skills to mend cars. The garage man says that if I provide him with spanners he will teach him. He is a lively boy. For three days he went missing. I thought he was in trouble. He had gone with a man who taught him to drive, although he has no licence. I told him, 'If you misbehave, I will chase you from the house, no matter how much I love you.'

My husband lives on the coast. He has other wives. Sometimes he sends me money, so he contributes towards keeping the children.

We were not happy about moving here in 1974, but we had no choice. We had to leave our oranges and coconut trees. The government introduced poultry-keeping, tailoring, cows, and gave us 15 acres to farm communally. The intention was to sell what was harvested and distribute the rewards according to the amount of work done by each. If 20 people were designated to go to work on a particular day, less than ten would appear; the others said they were sick or had family problems. In any case, the money disappeared. We were given a ten-ton truck, but it was sold. The most powerful people took the land for their own use.

Asha wakes at five o'clock and, after prayers, cooks breakfast. In the busy season, she prepares the food for the whole day, and works from early morning until nine o'clock at night, tending, weeding, harvesting her crop of maize and rice.

She never went to school. She can read a little Arabic, having spent some time in a *madrasa*. She does not know how old she was when she married. 'In those days, parents watched the development of a girl, and when she began to menstruate they started looking for a husband for her.'

At bedtime, Asha tells the children stories. She tells of a grandfather who had two wives and brought up two families – one that was loved and one that was not. The children of the unloved family went to another woman who cared for them tenderly. This is their favourite story.

She teaches the children a humane and tolerant Islam – to love others, respect elders, lead honest lives, not to 'run here and there' – that is, not to be promiscuous.

> I am sorry for the young people. They have temptations unknown to us – alcohol, drugs, bhang. Of course, marijuana was always there. It grew wild, and we used to eat it as a vegetable, because it is nutritious. Our elders drank beer only at festival times. Now young people want stimulus – they drink *gongo*, fermented from papaya, cassava and sugar cane. It is strong and cheap. It helps people pass on their pain to another day.
>
> I am thankful I have someone to look after. There are too many lost children. They did not choose for their parents to die. I pray every day that I will live long enough to see them all reach adulthood, to develop the skills they can and to respect all human beings.

Today is the first day of Ramadan. Asha is preparing the *iftar* snack, with which they will break their fast after sundown. The youngest children do not fast because they are too small, but the older ones observe what she has taught them.

The November rains are late: a vigorous shower falls noisily on the metal rooftops of the hut, dripping off the plantains and acacias, and scattering the children playing in the dirt yards.

The catastrophe of AIDS is mitigated, not by promises of a phantom 'international community', but by the courage and tenacity of millions of older women who have become carers of the terminally sick, yet from whom a global market capriciously withholds basic drugs in the name of freedoms which they do not understand.

THE BURDENS OF THE ELDERLY

For many people in the world paid labour, the work of self-provisioning, the necessary tasks for daily survival, including the care of the vulnerable, are not clearly demarcated. The elderly move easily between these different areas of vital work, and in doing so they bear a disproportionate burden of social labour. Discussions in the West about encouraging older people to work simply do not apply to the South. Indeed, if we look at the neglect of the potential of the young elderly in the rich world, and the abuse of old age in the poor world, we see a wasting of resources on the one hand, and a wasting of humanity on the other. The mirror images of idleness and exploitation are the two faces of a growing global injustice.

What both the West and the South have in common is that the elderly are themselves major providers of care for the weak and dependent. Old age is not static. Infirm people frequently look after those even more enfeebled than they are. Mutual support, in particular, between couples, enables them to continue to live independently for longer than would otherwise be the case: one may be immobilised, while the other is affected by memory loss; one may have a heart problem, the other failing eyesight. But by pooling their resources, they can sometimes complement each other's frailties and not become a burden, either on their families or on the state.

I spent much of the last few years of my mother's life in India. When I explained to people there that my mother was in a nursing home, they looked at me with an estrangement mingled with pity. 'How,' they asked, 'are such things possible? Why can other family members not take care of her?' 'There are none.' 'Then what are you doing here in India when your mother needs you?' I was looked upon as a defector from natural feelings, a refugee from humanity. I tried to explain that there was no one else to look after her, that we lived in a welfare state (what, they might have asked, but didn't, is that?), and the final, irrefutable argument that I had to make a living.

But the questions resonated. Why did I have to make a living in India? What was I doing, researching popular resistance to liberalisation in India, when at home we had put up such small resistance to the destruction of the *protectionism of flesh and blood* towards one another? That I had to work sounded more like an alibi than a necessity. And had my mother not constantly repeated the permission to desert her, by the resignation implied in the much repeated concession, 'You have your own life to lead'? At what point, I wondered, did the leading of my own life diverge so radically from my duty towards her? I found no answer to this question, not even in her death.

THE ENABLING STATE

The tug of war between the bonds of love and economic necessity is an ancient one, and in one form or another spares few people in the world. What is more, all the anxieties of old age that were to have been laid to rest by the welfare state are not banished, but rather refracted by it.

The 1908 Pensions Act in Britain set the age of eligibility at 70. Insofar as this was intended to provide security in retirement, it cannot be said to have been very successful, since most people didn't reach 70. It was set at well below subsistence level – between one and five shillings a week for those whose income was below twelve shillings a week. At that time, more than 60 per cent of men over 65 were still working.

Throughout the twentieth century, the official response towards the elderly has faithfully mirrored prevailing economic conditions. In the depression of the 1930s, politicians praised the willingness of older workers to be 'pensioned off', to make way for the young unemployed. By the 1950s, however, labour shortages ensured that older workers were retained, and their reliability and commitment were widely commented on. In the 1980s, with high unemployment once more, many older workers were 'made redundant' and retired early. Within the last few years this has been reversed once more, and a new scare about the ageing population has led to the 'crisis' which we are now supposed to be living through: the experience and steadfastness of the older worker are back, together with the generosity of a government which has outlawed compulsory retirement for those over 65. Raising the retirement age is politically impossible in the immediate future, since many older people suffered from an excess of labour. To speak of providing such people with further work opportunities will strike many as insensitive at best, and some will find it insulting. The legacy of industrialism is not so easily effaced as the mere demolition of mills and factories. In 2002, in Surrey in Southern England, the average years of healthy life expectancy stood at more than 72 years, whereas in Manchester it was only 61.

It is, perhaps, too easy to respond to alarmist and instant stories which will be forgotten the day after tomorrow: social transformation does not occur overnight.

There are, however, discernible shifts in attitudes towards the elderly, as a result of the establishment of the welfare state. After the Second World War, the principle of 'universality' was acknowledged in Britain, and entitlement to the old age pension and health care became a right, independently of means. The pension was still modest, but provision was made for supplementary payments to be made to those whose income fell below a certain standard.

Since it was widely recognised that for those with no other income, the state pension offered only a bare sufficiency, many workers also paid into company pension schemes, which would ensure that retirement would not bring penury. Poverty among the elderly persisted – neediness increases with age – but for a majority, the hardship and want that had characterised the old age of the survivors of industrial society ceased to exist in the extreme form they had taken in an earlier industrial age.

As the post-war economy flourished throughout the 1950s and 1960s, pensions continued to be graded upwards in relation to the average wage. In the 1980s, however, the Conservative government cut the link to earnings and indexed the pension to the level of inflation, which consistently remains lower than wages.

Mass unemployment of older people in the 1980s and 1990s and the growing numbers of very old were not perceived as a major threat to fiscal stability until the turn of the century, with three years of steadily falling stock markets, and the decline in the value of the assets of pensions schemes. It is in this context that renewed concern has been expressed over how the country will finance its future elderly. Half the companies that operated 'final salary schemes' had closed these to new entrants by 2002. This has exposed the fragility of dependency upon pension funds. Discussions have changed very quickly in response to the new situation. Individuals must expect to provide for themselves, by amassing, in one form or another, a 'pot of money' (the archaic language suggests treasure buried in the earth or the sock in the mattress) to secure a retirement free from want. That many people will never be able to earn enough to do this has led to dire predictions about the future fate of the elderly, the need to raise the retirement age and, maybe, to compel people to save.

This suggests a return to an earlier age when the worker was 'free' to negotiate his or her future as an individual with the capitalist system. Friendly societies and mutual self-help groups were founded throughout the nineteenth century in order that members might share responsibility for the contingencies of life

– it was impossible for individuals to do so. People came to see that only through collective action would a reasonable security be attained. It was only thanks to the solidaristic efforts of workers, their organisations and the exertion of political influence that universal pensions were achieved in 1948. It is an historic irony that the dismantling of that achievement, of making people safe against the vicissitudes of life – sickness, poverty and age – threatens to plunge people, even in the rich societies, once more into a similar, troubled uncertainty which haunted the starvelings of early industrialism, and which torments a majority of the people in the developing world today. It is almost as though we are witnessing the undoing of an epic struggle, the reversal of what seemed to many in the 1940s as an enduring 'settlement' between capital and labour.

In the light of this, the question often raised by people from poor societies about the faltering role of the family in the West in supporting the old and vulnerable takes on a new urgency.

The weakening of the sense of duty proper to kin is, no doubt, partly a consequence of the apparatus of welfare designed to cushion people against destitution. But the welfare state was itself a response to a driven and often violent industrialism which uprooted people, tore families apart, created a world of upheavals and migrations, in which the risk of dereliction remained high for the majority of those who had only their labour to keep them from extreme poverty. Through all the harshest visitations of industrialisation, the family remained the most powerful source of security.

The welfare state was intended to remove that fear of impoverishment, a terror that had hung over every working-class community in Britain since the Poor Law Amendment Act of 1834. The Gothic bulk of the workhouse, on the tympanum of which were inscribed the words 'The Poor Ye Have Always With You', shadowed the lives of the poor and insecure old. Under the law of 'less eligibility', the worst-off pauper outside the workhouse had to be better off than anyone housed within its austere precinct. The Act of 1834 was supposed to end all out-relief for paupers, although this was nowhere achieved. In the 1840s, it was estimated that almost 80 per cent of relief was still paid in pensions and allowances to those living outside the workhouse. A number of scandals enhanced the fear among the industrial population: at Andover in 1845, conditions were so harsh that inmates were found to have been eating decayed meat from bones they had been set to work to crush.

Although the actual percentage of people institutionalised was never very high (varying historically between about 3 and 7 per cent of the old), it served as a warning and example to the people; and stories abounded of the meagre fare, the punitive regime, the coarse uniform, and separation of the sexes – husbands and wives were segregated, and some are said never to have seen their spouse again after passing through its forbidding portals.

The welfare state was designed to erase this punitive past. Its comprehensive provision would ensure relief and welfare for the old and sick. It was, perhaps, inevitable that this would permit a certain loosening of the duties of family. It certainly gave greater freedoms to people, especially women, to pursue their own lives and careers. People could disperse in a new division of labour which often took them far from their place of origin. They felt it was safe to leave their dependants to the merciful administration of was called in the 1960s the 'caring society'.

These freedoms crystallised in a new individualism in which people were able, for the first time, to define themselves against the older collectivities of family, workplace and community. In the process, the structures of welfare, the very defences that had been erected against want and poverty became agents of further mobility, and moving away from home was no longer perceived as abandonment or desertion. People remained secure in the knowledge that those they loved would be guaranteed free medical and social care. This duly occurred; and it ensured the survival into old age of many who would have died in an earlier generation.

It has to be restated that this does not represent a dilution of feelings within families, nor even of the duties they perform for one another. It is that, in the altered social and economic context, duty is configured in a different way. You may not live in the next street, you may not take a widowed parent into your home, you may not see them daily, but tending them in a final illness, talking to them daily by telephone, taking them on holiday, seeing them at times of festival and holiday – these less intensive attentions are sometimes mistakenly taken to be signs of indifference. What can be said is that the social purpose of the old, their role as repositories of useful knowledge, their tutelary function, have decayed. This is sometimes blamed upon the callousness of the young. These are observable changes, but they arise from social and economic necessities which certainly create new social distances between the generations, but do not impair the affective and emotional lives of human beings, and do not prevent the majority of us from fulfilling the duties of kinship to the best of our abilities.

There has been, however, one important consequence for the pooling of risk represented by the creation of the welfare state. With the thrust of the ideology of individualism, the collective arrangements made for provision against the ills of existence come to be perceived as an onerous, even unbearable burden. Individuals came to feel that their contribution to the welfare of others, protecting them against misfortune, was an imposition rather than a necessary contribution to society. As the twentieth century wore on, the 'burden of taxation' began to appear as an unwarrantable interference with the liberty of individuals, and levels of resentment at 'punitive taxation' inhibited the rise in spending on services for those in need. Since providing for sickness and old age seems a nebulous and improbable venture (except to the sick and the old), it became the common wisdom that individuals should be able to spend more of their money as they chose; and since the young and vigorous determine the social mood, welfare nets were allowed to fray.

Under the impact of an ideology of individual heroics, life is seen more and more as a game of chance. The well-known capacity of the young and healthy to distance themselves from ageing and loss, and the faith of those in the prime of life in their own immortality come to dominate public discourse; while there are always at hand plenty of personal justifications for hardening attitudes. 'I won't live that long.' 'It may never happen.' 'You can have it all.' 'Tomorrow never comes.' 'You might get lucky.' 'Life is a gamble.' 'The bad times will take care of themselves.' 'Something will turn up.' 'They will invent something.' 'Life is what you make it.' 'If the worst comes to the worst, I'll take an overdose...'

In a context of perpetual optimism, where people have become tangibly richer, anything seems possible. It is perceived to be *wealth* that has delivered us from so many evils, not struggle or collective action; and the riches will continue to work their magic. More and more people are prepared to take their chances with life and whatever it has to throw at them.

THE PENSIONS CRISIS IN BRITAIN

In 2002, the British government confronted for the first time the dilemma over the economic reinsertion of the elderly. It was not that the ageing of the population came to them as a sudden revelation, but that the fall in the values of the stock markets threatened to reduce investments and had led to almost half the private companies offering 'final salary pensions' to their employees closing the scheme to new entrants. There was a widely advertised 'shortfall' in pensions of some US $40 billion.

The government did not propose to raise the retirement age, nor did it impose compulsory savings. But it abolished the retirement age of 65, and it declared that at least 3 million people are not saving enough for their retirement and a further 10 million are saving insufficiently to maintain a reasonable standard of living when they cease work. People were told they had to 'save more, work longer, or both'.

People who continue to work beyond 65 will gain an increment in their pension, proportionate to the length of time they carry on working after the statutory pensionable age. Legislation against age discrimination will be introduced by 2006. Future pensions are likely to be based on 'career averages' rather than on final salary.

This is regarded as the last chance to make a voluntary system of pensions work, although with the deficit in company pension schemes some form of compulsion seems inevitable. In Australia, the workforce and employers are statutorily obliged to provide sufficiently for retirement.

Alex Brummer wrote in the *Daily Mail*, 'The planned reforms do nothing to restore the dreams of millions who hope to retire and then cruise the Mediterranean, explore the Amazon or just enjoy the simpler pleasures of golf club membership and a cottage in Dorset.'

The government has recently provided a minimum income guarantee. This requires means-testing. Many believe it is a disincentive to those on low incomes to save.

It seems that the choice for Britain is either to raise taxes and, with them, the level of the state pension so that people can choose to save more if they wish; or to compel people to save more so that the great majority do not need means-tested benefits.

In 2002 one-third of people over 50 and two-thirds over 65 were 'economically inactive'.

THE RETREAT OF THE STATE

In such an environment, we discover that, almost by stealth, we are now compelled once more to make our own private accommodation with a global system in confronting the future risks in our life, in which old age, however much more likely it may be than in the past, nevertheless seems incredibly distant while we have all our lives in front of us…

This ideology found its most explicit expression under the government of Pinochet in Chile in the 1980s. Chile had had one of the most progressive social security systems in South America, funded by employers' and workers' contributions. Although it didn't reach the poor and the casually employed, it operated in favour of lower-paid workers and had a slightly redistributive effect.

When Pinochet overthrew the government of Allende in 1973, he abolished employer contributions. Then in 1980, following advice of the monetarist economics of the Chicago school, he privatised social security. Workers and employees who started work after 1982 were compelled to contribute to private pension funds. Those under the old system were offered inducements to transfer to private pensions. Privatisation required an increase in public funding, both to cover the deficit in the old funds and to subsidise contributors' payments to private funds.

The new private funds began collecting money instantly and were not required to pay out for a long time until the workers under the system began to retire. They became very rich, all the more so since one-third of all workers do not earn enough to have any pension coverage at all. After 20 years, 34 per cent of men and 45 per cent of women contributors will receive only the most basic pension, equivalent to 85 per cent of the minimum wage. Government will have to supplement this to bring it up to the level of minimum wage.

The top 20 per cent get more under this system than they would have done under state provision. The argument that it is a more democratic system is negated by the fact that three non-Chilean financial groups control two-thirds of the capital in the private funds.

While investments on the global stock markets were rising, it was suggested that this system should be adopted by the US. It is of a piece with the ideology that the individual and not the state should be responsible for her or his own financial future.

Despite the injustices embodied within the system, and despite the uncertainties following declining values on stock markets, governments everywhere are looking to this model as the answer to the pensions crisis. Traditional pay-as-you-go systems will be superseded by mandatory individual private accounts. Individuals will once more make their own arrangements with unparalleled concentrations of wealth and power in the world.

In this way, convergence seems assured between the fate of the people in the privileged countries of the West and the great majority of the people in the South, who have never known any provision in times of need that has not been furnished by the hands of family, however roughly they may sometimes have dispensed it.

It is an historic irony that, as people in the poor world increasingly recognise that what they most need is a system of solidarity against ageing, decline and loss of earning power, in the rich world they are being encouraged to make their own individual arrangements. In China, according to Zeng Yi, such an undertaking would be on a scale to match the construction of the Great Wall of China. Even Bangladesh, one of the poorest countries in Asia, introduced in 1998 a system of paying a small monthly pension (only 100 taka – US $2) to a limited number of elderly in each district, while India has a theoretical commitment to small payments to the elderly, although for most it is lost in the labyrinths of bureaucracy and corruption. Most of the poor world dreams only of building systems which the West not only takes for granted, but, in some cases, is prepared to undermine.

Chapter 3

> Anyone born in 1950 could expect to live 46 years, 34 per cent of the world's population were children, and 8 per cent were over 60.
>
> Anyone born in 2000 could expect to live for 65 years, 30 per cent of the world's population were children and 10 per cent were over 60.
>
> A person born in 2050 will expect to live 76 years, 21 per cent of the world's population will be children and 21 per cent will be over 60.
>
> There will be 314 million people over 80, 61 million over 90 and 3.2 million centenarians.
>
> (Source: HelpAge International)

WIDOWHOOD

Long life is not always a blessing; particularly for women who live on in long – and sometimes despised – widowhood. Except for a minority of privileged women, their lives are reduced in every way. They lose status, while at the same time they are expected to contribute to caring for those even older than themselves or making some contribution to the family income. A widow from Florida on vacation in Spain said to me that she felt widowhood was a kind of amputation. 'Part of me is missing and always will be. We were married for nearly 40 years.' She spent much of her life travelling – she was in her late 70s – but felt her wanderings were all a search for something she would never find, the peace and security of being loved.

On the gravestones of Britain, Victorian memorials describe widows as the 'relict' of the male, which suggests the relinquished, almost abandoned, the living remains, the trace of a defunct male.

In India, *sati* was officially outlawed by the British in 1834, when it was forbidden for women to immolate themselves on their husband's funeral pyre. Putting an end to this barbaric practice was held to be one of the most humane achievements of the colonial era. In the Bengal Presidency 8,134 women are known to have sacrificed themselves between 1811 and 1828. Yet the degraded status of widowhood remained; and in the late twentieth century, partly under the influence of fundamentalist Hindu revival, there have been a number of cases where women have tried to end their own lives at the time of a husband's funeral: one of the most notorious was that of Roop Kanwar in September 1987 in Devrala, Rajasthan, where the authorities forcibly had to prevent villagers from constructing a temple on the site of her sacrifice.

To discover how far the stigma of widowhood still pervades India, in September 2002 I went to Vrindavan in Uttar Pradesh, a city of widows.

A broad open space in front of a temple surrounded by high ochre-coloured walls. A spreading neem tree is the only vegetation, surrounded by a platform. A hundred or so women, most of them elderly, stand or squat in the shade, all in the white weeds of Indian widowhood, insubstantial as the eddies of dust which, stirred by the breeze, perform a ghostly dance around them. They have gathered around the mobile medical unit of HelpAge India, which visits Vrindavan once a week, offering free medical treatment to some of the thousands of widows who have come from all over India to finish their lives in this city of widows: wraiths with puckered skin and bones of bamboo.

Vrindavan is close to Mathura, birthplace of Krishna, and is part of the *braj*, the holy ground where he spent his childhood and youth, and where his dalliance with the *gopis*, the herdswomen of the countryside, is commemorated in countless paintings and carvings. The women who come here have done so in an ambiguous pilgrimage of religious exaltation and social rejection, since the ancient shame of widowhood lives on, and these women, elderly *gopis*, mutilated of their deceased lords, are its victims.

To die in this, one of the holiest sites in India, in devotion to Krishna is to do so in a state of heightened purification; and this must serve as a consolation for the more or less brutal eviction many have suffered at the hands of their families.

Most tell a similar story, of the joyous privilege of being in this sacred spot, but as they talk, tears splash the dust beneath them, and they are tears of grief, not gratitude. They spend the day chanting *bhajans*, devotional songs, in the surrounding temples, four hours in the morning, four in the afternoon. Each woman is paid two and a half rupees per session (a little under 5 US cents). They are given a metal token, which they can exchange for money when they have ten. The maximum they can earn is 10 rupees a day. Some can take their payment in food – 100 grams of rice or dal.

> Tulsi Chatterjee comes, like a disproportionate number of the widows, from West Bengal, where, traditionally, widows were forced to shave their heads to avoid provoking desire in men other than their dead husbands: a kind of posthumous policing of chastity. She came here six years ago, 'for the sake of religion. I had got my children married, two sons and one daughter, and now I have to find my own way into the other world. I don't want to leave here. Whatever the Lord Krishna gives, I am satisfied. I wanted to come many years back, when my husband died, 18 years ago. I travelled here alone. I fled, without telling my children where I was going. I thought, While I can still move independently, I should go. If I stay there and cannot move, I will become a burden and they will wish for my death sooner. I am 65. Children do not want to look after their parents. My daughter has visited here once, not my sons.'

> Sushila Mandal says she is 'about 60'. Her husband died twelve years ago. He was a landless labourer working on the land of others for a daily wage. She had two sons and two daughters, but her younger son is dead. 'I wasn't getting food at home. I lived alone. My older son wouldn't let me stay with him and his family. Nobody was there to take care of me. I am happy here. If you are not happy in Vrindavan, you will not be happy anywhere in he world. I recite *bhajans* eight hours a day in the Mirabai temple. I pay 50 rupees a month to the ashram where I stay, which leaves 100 rupees a month for food. I make my own meals, dal and roti. I do not beg on the streets, but what people give I accept.'

The medical unit of HelpAge India has been coming here for six months. For many, this is the first medical attention they have received in their lives. It has uncovered a picture of neglect, vitamin deficiency and malnutrition.

> Basunti Das says her whole body aches and she cannot see; the eyes of women are veiled by cataracts and tears. Many suffer breathing difficulties, infections, coughs and body pain, swollen knees and intermittent fevers that dehydrate and weaken. Kamla, 70, is from Mathura. She has one son who does not look after her. 'In any case, he drinks, so even if I am happy with him, I cannot stay there. This place is holy. Who cannot feel close to Lord Krishna, knowing she is in the *braj*?'
>
> Ramshree says she has no home. She is confused. She says she was born in Agra and has been here for 35 years, but then says her husband died 15 years ago. 'He had a shop, but when he died I had to come here, because my family do not take care of me. My sons do not even give me water, much less food. I cannot see with one eye and with the other I can see only shadows. Here I sing *bhajans*. I am killing time. When I remember my family, I weep. But I never forget I am living in the *braj* – nothing can go wrong here.'
>
> Lalabhai is from Ranga, about 50 kilometres from here. She is 70 and has spent eight years here since her children evicted her. 'Sometimes I eat once a day, sometimes twice, sometimes not at all. I have no place to stay, so I sleep in the temple. Even if I get money, I have no place to cook, no utensils. I have two sarees, that is all. I recite *bhajans* in the Radhessyan temple. I am frightened sometimes when the fever comes. There is no one to look after me in the temple. Sometimes' – she indicates the surrounding circle of old women, whose bright dark eyes glitter beneath their ghost robes and pale hair – 'my sisters help. When we are sick and incapable of helping ourselves, we must depend on the charity of sisters.'

Here are stories of extreme dereliction: women, married in early childhood, whose husbands died within months, or weeks, of marriage, ill-omened infant brides, culpable for having lost their men even before the marriage was consummated, and condemned to a lifetime in the exile of widowhood. A five-year-old, widowed after 20 days, is now in her ninth decade here.

Ramdevi is 65. her husband died of fever five years ago, and her sons took the land and threw her out of the house. 'My son said, "Go. You have nothing now. Your husband is dead. I need the land." He has one son. They never come to see me.' Ramdevi came to Vrindavan with her unmarried brother who is a *sannyasi*, and moves from place to place. She lives in Paresharam Ashram, where she pays rent of 100 rupees a month (US $2). 'I have a small room. Whenever I get food, I eat, but I cannot cook in the ashram.'

Hona has been here for two years. Her husband died eight years ago. He lost a kidney and the other failed. She has two sons, the younger of whom is mad. He is looked after by his brother, but Hona says she didn't want to be an added burden, so she left. No one comes to see her. 'Look,' she says, 'at the clothes I wear.' She says she is happy, but at the same time wipes the tear-stained cheeks with the palm of her hand.

Vidyadevi is 'over 60'. Her son married two women, but she cannot stay with them, because the older wife used to beat her. The younger one was kinder but was not in a position to maintain her if the older one forbade it. She came here six years ago. 'It is fate that has brought me here. If the Lord wants me to be hungry, I will be hungry, if he wants me to eat, I will eat.'

Rajamati is 68. From Gorakhpur, she has been here for five years. She sings *bhajans* eight hours a day. Today is *kadasi*, a day of fasting; with her thin, sunken face and faded saree, she looks as though fasting is the last thing she needs. Her children are in Delhi. Her son ordered her to go. She came with a friend who was in a similar situation. Rajamati was one of the few women who expressed the ambivalence of the feelings about being here. She gave some hint of how the women survive psychologically. 'I am not happy, who can be happy? I do not like singing *bhajans* for two and a half rupees or some food, but this is my luck. I suppress these feelings and put them somewhere else in my mind for some other time. Only in the night, they sometimes come back in dreams and I wake up crying.'

I went to the Aamar Bari Ashram ('Our Home' in Bengali), which was opened four years ago as a private charity by a woman who had been chairperson of the National Commission for

Women. Many ashrams are squalid and unhygienic. This is one of the best ashrams in Vrindavan, where all basic necessities are provided, including medicine and food. Each woman has her own tiny room, and all are devotees of Krishna. Whatever sins they have committed, here they have come to find *moksha* (absolution) since the earth here is purified and their wrongs will be washed away. Few of the hundred residents are visited by their children. There is in theory no discrimination here, but in practice only Hindus seek refuge here.

The regime relieves them of the necessity of having to chant for their food. They rise at five o'clock and prepare for the day. Breakfast at eight is varied – tea, *channa, upama, daliya*. At eight thirty there is a yoga class. This is compulsory, except for those who are bed-bound; and is followed by readings from the *Bhagavad-Gita*. HelpAge sends a mobile unit here twice a month, and their health is monitored. Lunch is at one thirty. Today is a day of *vrat* (fast), so the menu is modest – two buckets, one of rice, the other of thin dal, stand outside the kitchen. On other days, there are vegetables, rice, with cottage cheese and milk, and *khir* (a sweet milk pudding) twice a month. There are *pakoras* on special days, but the diet is strictly vegetarian, and excludes onions and garlic.

At two o'clock they clean the dishes and vessels, and wash their clothes. The more active assist the helpless, bathe and feed them. From two to four they rest. Then fruits are distributed. At four thirty there is tea, and from five to seven thirty meditation or *bhajans*. Dinner at seven thirty is followed by milk at eight thirty, and after that, the women sleep as they will. By ten o'clock the whole ashram is sleeping. Occasionally, there are video films – some devotional material, but also a Hindi film.

The ashram performs the last rites for the dying and the dead. Cremation is also taken care of. On the 13th day, the ashram feeds 13 Brahmins. 'People are happy to die here,' says Gita Pandey, who is running the ashram. She adds, 'Their relatives rarely come.'

This is one of the best maintained ashrams in Vrindavan. It is constructed around a series of courtyards, some of them two storeys high; pots of *tulsi* – holy basil – grow in pots at the entrance to each yard. The rooms are tiny cube-shaped spaces, no more than a couple of metres, small windowless cells with dark green doors. Above the central courtyard, a wire mesh prevents the ubiquitous monkeys leaping across the rooftops from stealing the food.

In spite of this, here I saw one of the most distressing scenes in Vrindavan. An old woman, almost 90, lies spreadeagled on a cloth on the floor of her little room. She is very ill. There is a saline drip in her arm. To prevent her from tearing it out, her hands have been bound on either side to two bricks – her feeble strength is not equal to moving them. The door is left ajar, and she lies silently in the gloom to await a death blessed by the holy ground.

On the other hand, here I also met Shapla Sundheri, a small, laughing woman in a green saree, who offered the most convincing account of religious joy.

Shapla is from a former royal family in what is now Bangladesh. The family moved to Tripura after Partition. She is now 72, but was only 14 when her husband died. She came to the ashram as a young woman. She was homesick and went back home, but returned to the ashram a few years later, 'because we are not people who remarry, because of our social position'. Her brother comes from Delhi to see her, and she visits relatives in the city. In her room, there is a bed raised about one foot from the ground, covered with brightly coloured bedclothes, with a little mat beside the bed. On a string there's a single change of saree. Shapla has built a shrine to Krishna: a little box covered with shiny gold and silver tinsel. Beside it, a seashell and some offerings to the god. Inside, a small lamp burns, and above, a picture of Krishna, and below him, a frieze of dancing *gopis*. In front of the shrine, she has placed a bowl of milk, some slices of coconut, a banana and some water in a metal tumbler. Today is a day of fasting, and she will break her fast with the food she has offered Krishna, purified by his presence.

Outside the ashram, Lokti Das was struggling up the marble steps that lead to the ornamental entrance. A tiny, frail woman in her late 80s, with big spectacles that magnify her eyes, she says she has been here for 60 years. She walks with the help of a rough wooden stave. She came here when her husband fled. Someone from the village gave her the money to travel to Agartala. She is very happy and likes all the food, 'except for

> groundnuts, because I have no teeth'. She says, 'No one remains at home. Everything is here. Give me your blessings, so that I may go in peace to the other world. We are waiting to die here, that is all. I am weak with pain and loneliness, but here you live on, so long you don't even remember how old you are.'

We sat in a restaurant in Vrindavan. The owner, a jolly rotund man close to 60, dressed in *khadi,* sat beside the till and the glass counter with its pyramids of sweets in gold and silver foil. He is Banshi Chatterjee, and he says,

> I don't want ever to leave Vrindavan, not even for one second of my life. I want my body to be burned here only. It is a blessing for the widows that they can come here instead of facing the consequences of being widows. To sing *bhajans* is good for them.
>
> We have our business here, which is at its best during Holi and Shravan Mahina, the rainy month, and especially at Janmasthami, which is the birthday of Krishna. In the rainy season, the temples are decorated with flowers, and people come from all over India to see that. There is one particular day, called Akhayatritiya, when the Lord sits in a golden swinging chair which is taken on procession all over the town. That day is like heaven. That is how heaven will be. I stopped wearing shoes 15 years ago so that I can feel the holy earth directly beneath my feet. In Vrindavan, 99 per cent of the people are very devout. There is a shrine in every house.
>
> We are living in the age of *kaliyug,* the time of destruction and disintegration. It will change again. But Vrindavan will remain, for here is the heart of the Lord Krishna.

As well as the piety, and the hope of the blessed death, Vrindavan is also haunted by stories of more material dereliction and abandonment. The small old faces beneath the neem tree are like a bunch of faded flowers: they are the ghosts of the measureless nurture and unrequited affection, the sacrificial love of women in all ages and societies. Their gestures of entreaty are unbearably poignant, a reproach to the constant ingratitude of those whose only advantage lies in having been born a little later than they were.

WITCHCRAFT AND OLDER WOMEN

In much of Africa, traditional animist societies have ascribed a very low status to widows. In some places, they have been regarded as responsible for the death of their husbands. Among the Igbo people of Northern Nigeria, widows were often expected to drink the water in which the dead husband's body had been washed in order to prove that they were not guilty of his murder. The head is often shaved, 'scraped' with a razor blade. The widow is regarded as defiled. She may have to sleep with the corpse as an enactment of a final sexual embrace. Her face is sometimes scarred. She may be forbidden to bathe and is unable to move out of the house. The widow is sometimes forced to chew a bitter nut, eat from unwashed plates for 28 days, and sit for long hours on the floor to demonstrate her abjection. She is occasionally obliged to have sexual relations with family members – brothers-in-law or father-in-law – in order to be free of evil spirits. This ritual is to sever all links between the living and dead.[1]

Naturally, WIDO, an international non-governmental organisation, is working not only to mitigate, but to eliminate such practices, but the work of cultural change is complicated by a number of factors, not least of which is the variety of systems of law operating – the constitutional legal system, Islamic law, customary law – and the way these interact to inflect local practice. Widows married under customary law are denied inheritance of land. In the Igbo culture women desperately want to produce sons, since only through them will they be able to have access to land and gain a measure of security.

The enactment of laws by central governments does not necessarily remove ancient and rooted customs. Culture is a living thing; campaigns against malign practices strike at the heart of people's beliefs and identities. If these are denied or forcibly disrupted, they may reappear in even more unacceptable forms.

Reports of witchcraft are common in the contemporary world, and old women are usually the victims. Most of these stories come from areas considered 'backward' or 'remote', from which the benefits of the modern world have been withheld. In Bihar in India (a state in which only 52 per cent of men and 23 per cent of women are literate), estimates of elderly women put to death for witchcraft amount to several hundred each year, despite a law recently enacted by the Bihar government requiring a prison sentence for anyone calling a woman a witch. Most witch killings have their roots in sickness or death. The village *ojha*, or exorcist, decides who is and who is not a witch. Mobs break open the doors of their huts and kill them, usually by hacking them to death.[2]

These stories – from Indonesia, Brazil, Tanzania – often originate in areas that, far from remaining untouched by the outside world, have been very profoundly affected by it; only the immediate cause of the dispossession they experience is not always apparent. In Bihar, many witch killings occurred in districts where the tribal Santhal people lived. Their habitat was the deep jungle, which provided them with everything they needed for survival – not only food and water, fodder and fuel, but also the *meaning* of the world. They worshipped aspects of nature, elements of the resource base which they sacralised, since it nourished their culture. When this was attacked, the forests were felled, first by the British colonial authorities, and later by the Forest Department of free India, the culture that depended upon the jungle began to fall apart.

The scapegoating of witches is part of the pathology of ruined cultures; aspects of tradition become both focus and agent of its disintegration. In addition to this, as the *Straits Times* report acknowledges, new diseases come in with the roads that are driven through the forests and open up closed communities to the outside world. Deforestation is a technical-sounding word, but it is also a violent assault on the fabric of the cultures of those who live there.

That this is a disordering of an older society is demonstrated by the fact that witches, in many societies, traditionally did not conceal their work. They were participating members of society – among the Maoris of New Zealand, the Quiche of Guatemala and many *Adivasi* (tribal) groups in India.

The power of witches comes in part from their position between this world and the next. What better intermediaries with the world of the spirits than the elderly who are so close to it? An animism that placates the spirits of water, trees, animals and birds, is no idle aberration: it reflects the dependency of the people upon the resources that sustain them. When these are degraded, it is neither the loggers and contractors nor the dam constructors and politicians who are blamed. The society turns inwards and seeks malefactors where they can be reached and punished. Since witchcraft has always involved a relationship with the natural world, it is not surprising that, when the natural world is under pressure, the failed intermediaries with the departed spirits should bear the blame and come to be seen as a malignant force in the world.

* * *

Around Mwanza in Tanzania on the southern shore of Lake Victoria, there was an increase in the killings of elderly women accused of witchcraft in the 1980s and 1990s. Witchcraft had always been part of the traditional animist culture, but it took on a more virulent aspect following the villagisation programme introduced in the time of Julius Nyerere in the 1970s. This shows how the consequences of what were intended to be wholly benign processes of 'modernisation' are actually perceived as an assault upon tradition and lead to an exacerbation of evils that are supposed to be eliminated by 'development'. That this occurred as a consequence of Nyerere's experiment in socialist self-reliance rather than, as elsewhere, the imposition of an IMF-inspired 'structural adjustment programme' makes little difference: it involves the disturbance of traditional societies. These had, in any case, been disrupted by colonialism and the imposition of a cash economy in place of ancient patterns of subsistence. It is simply that globalisation continues and intensifies the violence of the imperial era.

Balthasar Shitobelo works with MAPERECE, a group of elders in Sukumaland, where accusations of witchcraft have been most damaging and destructive. He links the killings directly to the process of villagisation and the introduction of national laws which gave widows the right to inheritance of land.

> Before the 1970s people lived scattered, far from each other, each with their own *shamba*. Before the colonial period, we had a barter system – cassava or sorghum. Cows were given as dowry – ten cows would be needed to buy a wife. Colonialism brought cash crops, but the social system remained the same. After Independence, the population in the villages increased.

New diseases began to appear or to be identified, such as tetanus or cholera. People believed that these had been caused by older people casting spells on those they wished to harm. Before the modern world, witchcraft had been a part of traditional religion.

It expressed the evil powers of the world. It was believed that a witch could take fire in her mouth and not be burned, could wash in boiling water without being scalded. They could also fly through the air. There were also good things in the tradition – healers who knew how to cure sickness with roots and herbs. In this area, there were many healers. The secrets of men made them healers, but the secrets of women made them witches. We used to believe in the sun and its power. Formerly, people looked to the east and prayed to the god who is the source of life. Liyuba is the sun god, without whose light life on earth is impossible. Some of the tradition was harmful. For instance, when twins were born, people sometimes threw them away because it was seen as a sign of misfortune. In the past, women had to dig the graves in the cemetery whenever there was an epidemic.

People were brought into close contact for the first time by being forced to live in villages. They came to know more about their neighbours. The government programme to build houses had created new enmities and jealousies. Some large farms were confiscated and redistributed to others – farms of 20 acres were taken by the government and divided up to share with others. When it came to the division of these smaller plots for inheritance, quarrels began between families. They looked for other ways of getting rid of those occupying land which they wanted.

Exploiting the fear of witchcraft provided an excuse. There would have to be some event which they could blame on some ill-wisher. When you are farming – say cotton or cassava – some people can use fertilisers, others cannot; some get a better yield. When the harvest comes, you can see the difference. We also believed that crops could be bewitched.

At first, they would accuse a widow, set fire to the house and tie the doors so that she would burn inside. Then tactics changed in the 1980s when killings by machete started. The idea of getting rid of the older woman originates within the family, but the killers are hired from among the unemployed youth. In nearly every village there are young people with no employment. These would be given money to perform the deed.

Traditionally, we respected older people. The forcible resettlement of people reversed the culture and young people began to say that killing the old was a good punishment.

But tradition is distorted by the modern world. New religions come. People's way of life has changed. The old beliefs do not die, but they also change. The leadership in rural villages comes from outside; old sources of authority break down. Village leaders become government employees rather than respected elders. They know nothing about our life, they cannot speak our language. Modern life does not stop the killings – police and bureaucrats cannot influence the way people think and feel. In any case, they are corrupt.

In earlier times, leaders knew how to handle this. A meeting would be called to punish the witch. The old woman who was declared to be a witch would have to offer a cow, and all those affected by her spells would share the meat. The 'witch' would apologise and there was reconciliation. Occasionally, they would be sent out of the community, ostracised, but never killed.

You have to work with the culture to change it. Now, cultural change is so sudden, people are bewildered and they fall back on older practices. If you say to people, 'Stop doing this', it will have a negative impact.

Traditionally there was a culture of burning people or beating them to death for theft or other crimes. Today, if you take them to the police, they will simply buy their way out. That is true all over the country – because of police corruption, when criminals are caught red-handed they are likely to be killed by the mob. The government system is unsatisfactory, so people think this is the way to deal with it once and for all.

We use traditional cultural forms to address the problem of witchcraft – social interaction, song and dance, educational drama – to teach that this form of killing or revenge is not good. Traditional healers also play a big part, because it is they who link people's sickness to this or that individual witch. A healer may be powerless to treat certain diseases, so if someone doesn't recover, they might say that the witch has come again and she must be killed.

Medical services in rural areas are also poor. What used to be free now has to be paid for. You need money or you must sell a goat, a cock, a hen. Poverty and poor services compound the problem of linking disease with malevolent people. That is much easier than explaining the medical reasons for illness, such as malnutrition and lack of hygiene. We have reduced the number of older women being branded as witches. But when there is a death in the village, people hold their own post-mortem. Who caused this? is the first question.

People have lost faith in the traditional culture because of modernisation, intermarriage, the coming of Christianity, the state government. It is no good just saying 'This is wrong', you have to offer people some alternative to their damaged beliefs. Globalisation, TV, values from outside, people uprooted and disoriented, the spread of AIDS – you must expect to see local cultures become fundamentalist in response to such outside influences. And the most vulnerable are the victims. That means women. Especially old women.[3]

* * *

Even in the Britain of the twenty-first century, widows tell some strange stories. The social experience of widowhood is not always met with the sympathy and comfort that the bereaved woman might have expected. It is, of course, less dramatic than that of widows in South Asia or Africa; but widowhood, and the anxieties and ostracism it engenders, are one of the most significant monitors of persistent discrimination and prejudice from which women – especially older women – continue to suffer, even in those societies which most vigorously proclaim their commitment to equality.

May Tennant, now 74, gives the following account of her own experience.

When my husband died, he was 69 and I was 67. I was devastated, because we had been together for over 40 years. You learn to live with grief. After a time, you think less about the loss and more about the good times you spent together.

But what I wasn't prepared for was the reaction of my friends, or rather, those I had thought of as friends.

We had visited their houses, played cards, gone on holiday together. Our social life revolved around our friends, other couples. But when you lose a spouse, you become bad news. You are punished socially for losing the one you love. People drop you. You get the commiseration up to the time of the funeral, people call and ask if you are all right. But after that, you don't get the invitations to dinner or to go to the theatre. You're an odd one out. You don't make up the even numbers.

You don't realise how far people have thought of you as a couple – there is something neat and convenient in being a pair. But to be on your own – that deserves punishment. Maybe it is because you remind everyone that the same fate is awaiting them, and naturally they don't want to think about it, so they drop you. Whereas I used to get two or three phone calls every day, by the time Dickie had been dead six months, I was lucky if the phone rang a couple of times a week, and then it was generally my daughter. I felt doubly bereaved – I had not only lost a lifetime's loving companionship, I had lost people I came to depend on.

Of course, after a year or two, somebody else loses her husband and she makes contact again. But you can never feel the same about them. You know they are not friends and never were. I didn't realise how shallow social relationships can be. I had to start afresh. I went to classes at the University of the Third Age. I rebuilt my life from scratch. When old friends contacted me after they had been bereaved, I couldn't respond. I felt cold because I had received nothing from them but coldness when I was in need.

It was a bitter lesson. But I have made a new life. And although, as you get older, you don't make friends easily, at least when you meet others who have been through grief and loss, you start at a deeper level than you do with those who want to pretend it cannot happen to them.

Although these sufferings do not have the intensity and cruelty of widows in other societies, culpability persists, an irrational feeling that a widow is guilty of some kind of negligence, which widowers rarely encounter, however resourceless and grief-stricken they may be when their wives die.

REMEMBERING...

Old people are often said to 'dwell in the past' or to 'live on their memories'. This may be yet another formulation by the young, who still have all their living to do. However that may be, there comes a point in the lives of most who live long when the past becomes richer than the future.

But the old also bear witness of the power of human memory, and its capacity to transmit not only values but stories, over time. About 25 years ago, I met a man who was then in his mid-90s, and who had been brought up in a conservative family in a rural area of Northamptonshire. Mr Baines was born in 1887, and his father in 1857. Mr Baines's childhood was saturated with the stories of his father's youth, especially about the powerful grandmother who had brought him up. She, in her turn, had told the boy in her charge much about her upbringing at the end of the eighteenth century.

As Mr Baines talks, he evokes again the world of his great-grandmother, and time is momentarily bridged – almost two centuries – by the profound and affecting power of love through time. It is clear that he feels he knows her, this strong and spirited woman he never met. She is to him a more real acquaintance than many of the people in the old people's home where he now lives. Her words reverberate through him. In his dark eyes, there is, too, the glint of the child he was as he listened with hungry delight to his father. He recounts the stories with great accuracy as he was told them, not departing by a detail from the information so carefully transmitted. The old man speaks with the slight rasp of the old country accent, but as he reports his grandfather's speech, the dialect intensifies; and as he calls forth his great-grandmother, the country burr thickens even more.

> In the early 1800s, there used to be a gospel tent in Northampton, where the Mission building stands now. It was an open piece of ground. There was a Methodist preacher, a man who couldn't read or write but who held the people spellbound with his voice. He would stand up and say, 'As I am lying on

my bed at night, I can feel myself being swept through the pearly gates, and I am being washed in the blood of the Redeemer, and my sins are washed away, and His blood leaves me whiter than snow.' And everyone would be carried away by his eloquence, and the whole assembly of people would be singing and moaning with him.

My great-grandmother was a young woman, and she and her friends used to walk the seven miles from the village of a Sunday night to hear this preacher in his tent. One Sunday, they'd been to hear him, I don't know which year, it was before 1820; it was a fair night, half moonlight, a bit cold, and as they walked home after the meeting, they were so full of the spirit of this preacher that they went singing hymns at the top of their voice. When they got to the village, they had to turn off the main road by the World's End pub, down a lane that led to the village. They were still singing as they went down the street, and separated one by one as they reached their homes. Grandma Baines lived down the bottom end of the village, in a courtyard where there were some cottages and some stables. So she was the last one to reach her house, and she had to cross a dark bit of street to get there.

As she was coming down, the ostler was going round the stables to make sure the horses were all right for the night, and he heard her coming. He'd been up the World's End that evening, and he was full of a different sort of spirit from those who'd been to the gospel tent. When he heard Grandma Baines, he thought he'd play a trick on her. He took the saddle cloth off one of these hunters, and when she turned in the gate to the yard, he let out such a groan it would curdle the blood. Of course, Grandma Baines, being full of the fighting spirit of the Lord and His works, when she saw this thing in the corner of the yard, had only one thought – it must be the Devil come to challenge her. So she stood her ground, and instead of running away she went at him, set about this ostler and gave him a really good pasting. He yelled out to her to stop. At the finish, he'd had enough. He got out from under the cloth and ran away over the fields. The next day of course the story came out, what had happened. But Grandma Baines wouldn't have it. Ever afterwards, as long as she lived, she insisted that she,

> single-handed, had taken on and fought the Devil. And not only that she'd fought him, but she'd won.[4]

In Western society this means of cultural transmission has been interrupted by the mass media, but the actual stories are not lost. They have all been recorded and stored by mechanical means. They exist in an imperishable archive, but no longer in human memory.

...AND FORGETTING

As more people live to be old, there has been a growing concern with various forms of forgetting – not merely the lapses of memory to which old age is prone, but to forms of erasure of memory, of which dementia and Alzheimer's disease are dramatic examples.

Forgetting is a very powerful metaphor. In spite of the intensive research that has gone into Alzheimer's disease, the element of genetic determinism, the power of Aricept and other drugs to delay its progress, the possibility of reversing it, this does not address the issue of the social context in which it has become so commonplace.

Soon after the collapse of Communism, Francis Fukuyama wrote about 'the end of history'.[5] He meant this in the sense that ideological struggle is at an end in a system which is supremely competent in delivering the goods: politics is no longer a matter of competing ideologies, but simply one of technical and administrative competence. This is the happy-ever-after of fairy tales, and it is a fitting belief for *a world grown old*. The world has indeed grown old, not only in the sense of the immense antiquity of the planet, but in the sense that its population is no longer predominantly young and impetuous, but has matured and stabilised. Since we know the secret of perpetual abundance, the rich societies are concerned only with living in the present, in the serene expectation that the future holds more, much more of what we have seen already.

It might have been expected that an ageing population would want to hark back to the past, to dwell in nostalgia. The contrary is the case. We can dispense with the past, upon which darkness has fallen. The past is the site of finished struggles and all the abandoned efforts to reach the supremacy of the present moment. History is strictly for consumption, fit for entertaining TV documentaries and costume drama, a source of academic occupational therapy. It has the power to thrill and distract, but bears no relation to the comforts which render our own past unintelligible to us. We have turned our back on all that. We live in a post-industrial society. The mills, mines and factories, nourished with human labour and sacrifice, have disappeared. They have been demolished, the spaces where they stood have been levelled and landscaped and prepared for luxury homes, malls and conversions. Of course, the experience of those who lived through those times has all been meticulously recorded, the oldest survivors have confided their secrets to the tape recorders of local history sections of libraries, the sepia photographs of *the way we were then* have been published and distributed in every town and city in the land. All has been told. The old have nothing more to say. They, like the rest of us, have been overtaken by new urgencies, the beguiling compulsions of the future. They have been used up, just as the rusted and silent looms, the exhausted coal seams in the derelict pit villages, the machinery that has been sold off to the factory in Mumbai or Kolkata. They have nothing to teach in the long future that beckons.

What could be more appropriate than that they should collude in the forgetting of archaic struggles and the defunct passions that once animated them? The world doesn't want to know. The world is listening too attentively to the voices and sounds in the air that speak of the next fashion, the newest trend, the latest celebrity plucked out of obscurity and headed for stardom, the winner of the jackpot, the wisdom of money. What can the old possibly say that is of significance to a people, born – or even reborn – under the universal though extra-zodiacal sign of the universal market?

And, as if to comply with this judgement, who can say whether the old do not acquiesce in the forgetfulness to which the times have also consigned them? They mimic, as it were, the very society which expunges the inconvenient remnants of discarded wisdom, erases memory, frames the lived experience and makes of it a curiosity, a diversion at best, certainly of no conceivable value to the way we live now.

Forgetting is a characteristic of old age; some form of dementia affects one in ten of those over 65 and one in five of the over-80s. It is only natural that the elderly, bypassed and ignored, should yield to the temper of the times and fall silent on the past, that shrouded land from which we are all refugees.

This is to some extent borne out by the evidence: far from the next generation eagerly absorbing the knowledge of its predecessor, the old increasingly imitate the young. The hedonism of old people in Japan, Europe or North America can be very touching. There is, after all, something heroic in the desire to keep ageing at bay, to be part of the modern world, to enjoy yourself while you can, *to get as much out of life* as possible. This is often a positive response to ageing, but if it leaves people without resources when the time comes to confront infirmity or debility, it becomes something less admirable.

I once visited a hospice where a woman who was to die later that day was having her hair done. She sat in the chair, her gaunt face staring back at her, the floss of silver hair beautifully set, and a powerful affirmation of life at its very end. The smile she gave herself was already the smile of a ghost. It was a profound and unforgettable experience.

It is never easy to strike the balance between holding on to life in the present, however diminished, and giving due weight to the past. The memory of the old is increasingly colonised by commerce, filled with fragments of manufactured culture rather than direct experience – bits of old TV programmes, snatches of pop songs, the inert remembrance of things consumed, a heritage of ashes, junk culture as unmemorable as fast food. Amnesia becomes a refuge from a past that has crumbled to dust; and from there to dementia is a short step.

The frequent occurrence of forgetting among the elderly in the rich societies is said to be a reflection of increased longevity. This is, no doubt, true, but it is difficult to believe that there are no other social factors which contribute towards the phenomenon. Just when a whole generation have abandoned the unwanted recollections of hardship, struggle and want, stuffed into the cellars and attics of memory, unwanted by those to whom they might wish to offer it, forgetting becomes something more than a symptom of passing time.

There are, of course, clearly detectable physiological symptoms of Alzheimer's disease, which occurs in all societies. But in some of these, the affected person may be borne up by flesh and blood that disperses the weight of the burden and makes it lighter. Dr Shubha Soneja of HelpAge India was formerly a clinical psychologist. She believes that dementia or Alzheimer's disease can be more readily contained within the extended family in India.

> I had one patient, a woman, who became obsessed with the idea of going back to the place where she had been married. She no longer recognised anyone, not even her immediate family. But whenever she expressed this wish, some family member was always there to walk her a couple of hundred metres, and tell her they had indeed reached the place she wanted to visit. She was happy with that and believed what she was told. We prefer to call it a memory problem. We don't want to pathologise, to medicalise or to patronise old age. Of course, there needs to be several people to surround the affected person so that it doesn't become too much.

The presence of those who can share the responsibility of attending to the old woman's needs is a very different story from that of individuals when there is no other help. The testimony of Jim Grieves could not be further from the example given by Dr Soneja.

> Elsie Grieves started to forget in her mid-60s. She, like her husband, had been a factory worker in Nottingham. They had two children, one of whom had gone to university – the first in the family to do so. All had moved away from home and had responsible jobs. They rarely went home, but Elsie and Jim spent a week with each every summer. The pictures of the seven grandchildren stood on the little table by the gas fire in their third-floor council flat.
>
> At first, it was little things, but very soon, the words for everyday objects would not come. Older memories were more tenacious – growing up poor in a rented house, hiding with her mother in the cellar when the rent collector came, the feast of a penny bloater on Saturday night, the outside privy where you had to beat a bucket with a stick to frighten off the rats when you went out in the dark.

> Soon, even the immediate past was no longer recoverable. There was a period – the worst, according to her husband – when she knew what was happening to her, a look of fear and disorientation in her eyes. Then came anger against Jim, unreasonable rages and tears. Then came the forgetting of people, not her husband and children, but neighbours and acquaintances. It was only later that she no longer knew her immediate family.
>
> Jim took care of her, made sure she didn't wander away, took her by the hand. To some degree, she was able to perform actions that had become almost mechanical, as though memory were a physical, rather than mental, activity. After a few months, she lost the recognition of her children and then her husband. When the grandchildren came, she would say, 'What are these children doing here?' Jim carried on for almost a year, cooking and cleaning and attending to her. She followed him everywhere, afraid to let him out of her sight. One night she went out into the street and was almost run down by a car.
>
> She went into a home at the age of 71. She didn't recognise anyone for the last eight years of her life, and after two years in the home she lost the power of speech. She lived for five years, mute, knowing no one.

In the West, as well as a crisis in generational renewal there has been *a depopulation of the heart*, whereby problems become personal and individual. Absences surround the suffering person, the unchosen, even involuntary, desertions of flesh and blood. It is inevitable that such maladies will be exacerbated in societies in which everyone has become too busy, and individual survival has taken over from family or group survival.

That so many people try to contain by themselves the lonely and incessant pain of caring for those they love says much about the heroism and unacknowledged strength of those who do cope, even at great personal cost. I spoke with Lilian Tucker, now 82, who cared for her husband, Les, until his death.

> I've dealt with a lot of old people all my life, so to look after my husband was a natural thing to do. I knew before the doctors did. They pooh-poohed the idea, until I had to get very tough. He was conning them. We had been married 61 years,

we knew what each other was thinking. We were always able to discuss everything.

They forget where things are, that's the beginning. I put labels on all the kitchen drawers and cupboards, I hadn't spoken to him about it. He said, 'What's all this?' I said, 'You're getting forgetful.' He said, 'I'm not quite an imbecile yet.' I took them off again.

He knew all about it. It was like what his mother had. They called it senile decay then, they didn't understand what they do now. Alzheimer's gives it a more medical name, people can accept it better. I nursed his mother for four years.

Leslie was the earner. He had his own shop. He died in June 2001. He had a wonderful death. He had gone to the day centre, and he was jiving with one of the old ladies in a wheelchair, and he collapsed. I was out shopping. He had an aneurysm that burst. He lasted two days, and was kept pain-free. A year earlier X-rays had revealed he had cancer of the lungs. I didn't tell him. I said no to chemotherapy. He was then 83. I had nursed his father with a colostomy.

He went to the day centre twice a week, which gave me some respite. He used to repeat things. I had to blank him out at times. He'd say, 'You're not listening.' I had all the patience in the world. He was such a nice chap, full of fun and laughter. I have good memories.

Three quarters of an hour before he died, I sat beside him. I said, 'My feet are cold.' He said, 'Put them under the bedclothes.' The nurse came along to give him an injection. He said, 'No, you're not, I'm with my wife.' He died half an hour later.

It wasn't the Alzheimer's or the cancer that killed him. He'd taken Aricept, it doesn't cure it, but it keeps it steady. People are living longer, that's why you hear so much more about it now. A lot of people have come to me and I can explain it to them. I had a neighbour who became really spiteful with it. That didn't happen to Leslie.

I said we'll lead a normal life. We'd always slept together. I didn't get much rest, so I bought single beds. That was like the end of the world. It lasted two nights, then we put them together. They get frightened with it, they've got to have someone there to touch, reassure them.

If you can talk about it to them in the early days, some of it does go in. Les and I were fortunate. I explained to friends and neighbours. I said, 'He does forget.' I made a joke about it. I had good friends. He couldn't drive. He forgot where he was going. He used to write things on his arm – who the Prime Minister is, what day of the week it was. You had to try and cover up for him.

The best thing is to treat them as normal, but with more love and understanding. A lot of people grow apart instead of keeping together. I had two sons. One was killed when he was 17. You learn to live with things.

I get my strength from the family. My grandmother was a help in the street where we lived, she used to lay people out, put pennies on their eyes. Young people are not taught about death. You grow up to know what is what. My grandfather used to bring animals into the world, and I watched my grandmother. Nothing was dirty. I was brought up to help people without expectation of reward. That doesn't happen these days.

SEX IN OLD AGE

An old man who was badly affected by dementia was taken on holiday to Spain by his wife. He had ceased to know her. She had to do everything for him. In the shower, he turned to her and said, 'Who are you, you're a lovely piece of stuff,' and he tried to have sex with her without a glimmer of recognition. Simone de Beauvoir calls this 'erotic delirium', which sometimes affects those with Alzheimer's.[6]

To younger people one of the comforting myths about their elderly is their sexlessness. The idea of a tranquil renunciation of physical desire by the old is calculated to comfort them that older people are 'past all that'. As the women sometimes used to say in the street where I grew up – mystifyingly to a child – 'I've done my bottom button up for good.'

This denial is perhaps an extension of children's need to desexualise their parents. Children find – paradoxically – inconceivable the very act by which they were conceived. Sexual activity among the elderly is often considered disgusting. The stock character of the 'dirty old man' has been a figure of fun down the ages. Women do not arouse the same revulsion, mainly because they are placed in the popular imagination even further from carnal desire than men, in whom the persistence of sexual need is seen not only as revolting but also as slightly menacing.

The power of this cultural cliché no doubt contributes towards the abandonment of sex by many – the power of public opinion has its effect. And indeed, for some people interest wanes, while for others, although the response to erotic stimuli may be slower and genital sex less frequent, it is quite wrong to think of older people as asexual. It may be that fantasy or pornography play a larger role. I have met many older people who continue sexual activity with a lifelong partner. One woman told me, 'When he turns to me in bed, I feel the same as I did 40 years ago. No, not the same. It is a way of continuing to affirm our relationship. It never stopped. Why should it?'

One consequence of the denial of men's sexuality may be seen in the growth of sex tourism. In Thailand, where two-thirds of tourists are lone males, a high proportion are in their late 50s or older. Many say quite openly that the reason for their long journey in search of sex is the feeling of disapproval any expression of their need meets with in the Western countries. This is an outlet for older men; I know of no similar facility for women. Elderly men report that there is no expression of revulsion by the young women (or young men) with whom they develop relationships. Here is what a 71-year-old German man said:

> Of course, you know to some extent that it is play-acting. You know the money is the main factor, at least in the beginning. That doesn't mean they are being false or are bad people. Maybe a woman working in a bar is providing for a whole family back in the village. Thai women know how to make you feel good. They never turn you away. They are always ready to become a girlfriend, at least for as long as you stay in Thailand. I met Daeng seven years ago. After I retired, I went to Thailand for a month. I just took to her, and now, every year, she is there waiting for me at the airport. For the past four years I've being going twice a year, a month each time.
>
> The family live in a wooden house in Korat, they have some chickens and pigs. It's very crude. When we go there, I always take plenty of food, and I leave a few thousand baht when we leave. Daeng has never shown any sign that she doesn't like

me. Her face lights up whenever we meet. I know she has other such friends, but what she does when I am not here I don't care. She makes me feel 25 year younger. She makes me feel I am still a man.

My wife and I separated 20 years ago. I had forgotten what it is like to be held in the night, to feel someone close to you, warm and breathing. It has brought me back to life. I was living in the shadows. I know this is her work, I understand that. But I could not imagine it would ever happen in Germany. I feel sad that in my own country this would be impossible. Of course there are prostitutes, even Thai women. But there is no tenderness with sex workers in our country. They despise you, perhaps because they despise themselves. Here they don't. Daeng has a high regard for herself. In a way, she is always out of reach. I can't speak the language. We don't have intellectual conversations. When we are not in bed, we do separate things – she sees her friends and goes shopping, and I have my own friends, expatriates, people from all over the world who have gone to live in Thailand because this is where they can get what is not available at home. We talk, drink and go out for a meal.

I have been with sex workers in Europe, in Hamburg, Amsterdam. They are like machines. Thai women have the human touch.

Although there is no evidence that desire in women disappears with time, the idea of a 'dirty old woman' is virtually non-existent. There are, of course, physiological changes that affect both men and women in later life. This is sometimes discussed in the media in a mechanistic way.

A large part of the *Observer* magazine devoted to ageing, carried this paragraph on the sexual functioning of men over 60.

The great news for men in their 60s is that the penis has staying power (at least when they're asleep). Under 40, he has 4.2 night-time erections which last for a total of two hours and 20 minutes. At the age of 60-plus, he has 3.5 night-time erections, which last for one hour 55 minutes. Sadly though, the angle of that erection is sinking: from 20 degrees above horizontal at the age of 30 to 25 degrees below at the age of 70. And even better, just over 20 per cent of men his age

> experience problems achieving or maintaining an erection during waking hours. (And if he can't, that's what God made Viagra for.) Erections apart, he might find it that bit harder to get a good night's sleep. OK, he doesn't need as much nowadays, but if he has sleep apnoea (when he briefly stops breathing then starts again with a snore) it will be fitful and unrefreshing. And that enlarged prostate may be forcing him to get up and pee two or three times in the night now.[7]

This could only have been written by a young person; and it explains why a majority of people in Britain who say they have been victims of discrimination cite ageism as the cause (38 per cent). The lofty and amused sense of distance suggests that the writer regards the elderly as a different species, worthy of a kind of anthropological detachment. It exhibits the intolerance and contempt of those secure in the knowledge it can never happen to them; a sad comment on the discontinuities in human solidarity induced by a culture which segregates people by age, colour, religion, gender and sexual orientation. What the author of the *Observer* article says is true, of course. But the presentation of that truth is marked by a clinical absence of sympathy.

Men do take longer to achieve an erection, the power of orgasm may decline, the volume and intensity of ejaculation decrease. For women, the lessening of oestrogen after the menopause may result in a loss of vaginal lubrication, which may make intercourse painful. The vagina may become less elastic, but it is well documented that women are less prone to sexual dysfunction than men. In *Old Age*, Simone de Beauvoir says, 'A woman of 70 is no longer regarded by anyone as an erotic object.'[8] Older women have continence thrust upon them.

To some extent, this is changing in the West, where women like Joan Collins have famously prolonged an aura of desirability into their late 60s. The point about this, though, is the effort that has gone into the retention of an appearance of youth. Tom Kirkwood, author of *The End of Age*, an authority on the cellular ageing process, is credited, in the same issue of the *Observer*, with developing the 'disposable soma theory' which proposes that 'our cells age because of limitations in energy investment in maintenance and repair'. This mechanistic approach to humanity – the obvious analogy is with the motor car – does little for the real needs of the elderly which are articulated with far more tenderness by the real experts, the elderly themselves.

> Rita is 80, and lives in South London. 'I don't want to pretend I'm fifty. Nor is it sexual satisfaction as you get older, it is the importance of having someone to hold you, to make you feel cherished and loved. I enjoyed intercourse until I was about 70, but it was much less frequent than in the early days of our marriage. But desire, even passion is still there – I think fidelity is partly a question of remembering, remembering what it was like in the beginning, and keeping true to that even when you grow older. Especially when you grow older. He is still for me the boy in the soldier's uniform, the cigarette in his mouth, the cheeky smile I first saw in 1943. An outsider would have to look hard to see he is the same person. But I have that picture of him locked in my heart, and it has the power to move me every day of my life, even now he is gone. There isn't a day that goes by without speaking to him, not morbidly, I just tell him the things I've been feeling during the day. I know he hears me, and that comforts me. He hears me, not because I believe he's in heaven – I'm no judge of that – but because his presence is inside me.

With age, sexuality often shades into an affectionate physicality; the need for tenderness and a feeling of being cherished, acknowledged and *understood* do not diminish over the years. Indeed, these things are the most powerful defence against loneliness. As we grow older, the certainty that loss will occur makes the affirmation of one another a more vital part of the life of partners, with or without sexual activity.

The other side of this alertness to the possibility of loss is taking the other person for granted, becoming accustomed to his or her presence when habit may dull the sense of fragility as time goes by. Many older people are pierced by a sense of regret, 'Why did I never adequately express what I felt, my love and devotion?' 'You only realise when they're gone' is a common refrain.

A woman in her 80s said,

> I woke up one morning and said to him playfully, 'Where's my cup of tea then?' He always got up first and we sat in bed with tea and biscuits before starting the day. He didn't move. I gave

> him a little shove. Then I knew he was dead. I can't forgive myself for being so thoughtless. My last words were a reproach, even though he never heard them.

Loss of a partner late in life sometimes sends people in search of a replacement. Reports of remarriage among the elderly are mixed: the bereaved person seeks out someone who reminds him or her of the lost loved one. This frequently leads to unhappy marriages where resentment that the other person is not the dead partner ensures that the new relationship doesn't stand a chance.

Simone de Beauvoir reviews a number of literary and artistic figures who retained their sexual powers until late in life.[9] They are nearly all men, and more often than not, their interest is in much younger women. Goethe was attracted to young women, and in his 70s, he proposed marriage to Ulrike, who was 19: his son and daughter, fearing, perhaps, for their inheritance, intervened. Goethe subsequently renounced sex. In later life, Victor Hugo turned to prostitutes, although his interest was mainly voyeuristic. He took Marie Mercier as his mistress when he was 69. H. G. Wells was 60 when he fell in love with Dolores, and discovered he had unsuspected sexual powers. At 66, he broke with her, and then met the girl he called Brylhil, the most violent passion of his life. Michelangelo wrote passionate sonnets to Tommaso Cavalieri, whom he met when he was 57. Andre Gide recalled passionate sexual activity in his *Journal* when he was 75.

The desexing of the old is part of the diminished humanity attributed to the elderly: they are treated as a problem, a looming threat, a social difficulty to be managed rather than an opportunity to make use of their capacities and resources constructively for the rest of the people.

AGEING AND SEXUAL MINORITIES

It is a common belief that older lesbians, and especially gay men, suffer from loneliness and abandonment in old age. The implication is that, without families and having led lives in pursuit of sex, they are left high and dry as they get older.

In the summer of 2002, I spent two weeks in Brighton, where there is a considerable community of lesbians and gay men. I spoke to older gay men in particular, since when they were young any expression of their sexual orientation was criminal. A recurring theme among the elderly all over the world is the transformation of the social world and the values they were born to. Even when there have been spectacular material improvements, the scars of other archaic values remain.

Brighton 2002. The glassy staircase of waves breaks on the shingle. An old man hugs his windcheater and looks with wintry blue eyes on the mist that hides a blank horizon. He remembers a youth that was criminalised and a shame that could not be effaced by reforming legislation. 'Brighton,' he says bitterly, 'is a place for companionless old men.'

Others tell a different story – one of friendships forged in the adversity of prohibition, the trust developed in a time of shared outlawry, which have lasted into old age.

How easy it is to dismiss the sufferings of an unenlightened pre-history of the day before yesterday! The elderly man, frightened, literally, to death by a heart attack in a public lavatory when three policemen leaped out at him from the cleaning cupboard; the two women who lived together, but were so frightened that their relationship might become known that they never went out together and even went to the cinema on separate evenings. People remember the constant alertness to the signals of the 'friends of Dorothy', the signet ring and the eye movements more expressive than those of a *kathak* dancer, an undetectable kinship in a hostile world.

None of it matters now, not even to the elderly victims who, in their youth, negotiated life as though it were a perpetual underground. When they speak now, they do so with a candour that appears naïve to the contemporary sensibility. 'Of course, I was always a mother's boy.' 'My mum was my best friend and sweetheart, I never had a pal to equal her.' Dutiful sons recall how when, weakened by infirmity, she moved into the flat with them, was given the ornate bedroom with the view of the sea, how grateful she was for the tray with the doily she had crocheted and the red dahlia in the little vase to accompany the meal she could no longer eat. 'The doctor in the nursing home told her she had cancer on the day before she died. But the post-mortem found it was an occlusion of the stomach, which had been brought on because she let herself get dehydrated after the staff scolded her for wetting the bed.'

My mother was 91 when I told her I was gay. She cried a little, but then forgot all about it. I wanted her to know me for someone I was rather than for something I was not.

My mother never knew. I used to think if I tell her it will kill her. But I think she knew anyway. Not that she ever spoke a word about it, but she had a knowing of the heart that didn't need to spell things out.

I look at the young men in the bars and clubs. They look as if they don't have a care in the world. They throw parties to celebrate a love that has lasted six whole months. The young don't even look at you. Their glance slides over your face like a bucket of cold water. For them you are the walking dead. Age is something that will never happen to them. I wonder if the friendships we made are more lasting than theirs will be? Or doesn't it matter any more?

I thought I was so peculiar no one could ever love me – I always ended relationships before my partner did, these were pre-emptive strikes against being abandoned, which is what I felt I deserved. I despised men who were attracted to me, because I knew I wasn't worthy of it.

Being gay when it was a secret made me more independent. I have relatives, but I have grown distant from them. Friends you can trust, but family always have some other agenda lurking behind their acceptance. They want to convert you, make you normal, desexualise you. But friends acknowledge who you are.

The only reference to homosexuality I heard when I was young was my uncle talking about somebody who had been nicked for indecency in our town. He said, 'Turd-burglar, that's what he is.' Just the sort of image to provide the role model you're looking for at 15.

First time I ever went into a gay pub was the Trocadero in Birmingham. I stood there with one beer for about two hours, wondering what you had to do to talk to somebody. Just before closing time, a really nice young guy came up to me and said, 'What's the time?' I said, 'There's a clock up there.' I went home and cried.

It makes me jealous to think how easy it is now to be gay. I think I have been unfulfilled, emotionally and sexually.

I went into the army, and then I worked in a boys' settlement in the East End. I wouldn't have dreamed of touching any of them, although I was surrounded by temptation. As a result I had a breakdown at the age of 30. Today, being gay is not something to have a breakdown over, but it sure was then.

The young don't know what they owe us. I went to New York in the early 1970s. On Christopher Street, I saw men holding hands, kissing on the street, in broad daylight. It was a revelation to me. I knew I had to bring it home, and I became part of Gay Liberation. It was such a short time, after Stonewall and before AIDS, but it was the time of my life. Liberation was snared by commerce. Of course, I'm glad the outlets exist, but there is no memory of the struggle we had. I was talking to a young friend about the *Gay News* blasphemy trial, how we marched, collected money for the defence. He had never heard of it.

What do you do with desire as you grow older? Books. I get vicariously involved with the characters in a gay novel. Theatre, music, friends. Especially friends. Of course, elective friendships don't always survive sickness and old age, but family duty can also be thin fare when you are in need.

It is an anguish coming to terms with the fact that you can no longer go to bars and discos – well, you can, if you don't mind rejection and derision. They think old age is a disease. People used to think being gay was a disease, so it's come full circle – there's a creepy sense of déjà vu.

At night sometimes, you have these moments of fear. If I'm sick, if I have a stroke, if I can't get to the phone. I have friends who call each once a day just to check. You build up friends over the years, unconsciously maybe, you know one day you're going to need them. My dread is going into a nursing home, being infantilised and heterosexualised by the staff. I know one guy who keeps a cocktail of drugs to make the quick exit if the moment comes.

Research in California confirms that elderly homosexual men and women are no less well socially supported than their heterosexual peers.[10] The only difference is that they derive greater sustenance from friends than from families. The research does not confirm the stereotype that they are more socially isolated or depressed than elderly heterosexuals. The authors state, 'Empirical evidence of the impoverishment of gay and lesbian social networks for any age group is non-existent... In non-elderly samples, homosexuals and heterosexuals tend to receive social support, but from different sources.' 'However,' the report continues, 'we cannot assume that support from friends has the same effects as support from family. The differential significance of various support sources on psychological well-being is still unknown. To make the assumption that social support from relatives is more important to psychological well-being than support from friends may obscure valuable information about the resiliency, coping and family or kin networks of the older population.'

'THIS IS NOT MY WORLD'

The question of how far *social* change leaves elderly people stranded and isolated has so far – like so many other areas of ageing – received only slight attention. It is acknowledged that older people 'cannot adapt'; they are described as 'dinosaurs' or 'survivors'; they are frequently 'left behind'. A neighbour of mine, a very alert and smart woman of 88, said, 'This is not my world.' She meant that the values which she saw as having characterised her early years were no longer appreciated. 'Discipline, courtesy, respect for people. Of course, I suppose young people accept the world as they find it. We did. Perhaps they will be saying similar things in the years to come.' This came from a woman who had been a Tiller girl in her youth ('Mrs Tiller was very strict with us') and who had lived in Sudan for twelve years; her husband had died at 54 and she had worked until she was 60, so she had always prided herself on being forward-looking.

In the West, where people have been to some extent cushioned against the material asperities of change, the sense of being overtaken by alien values expresses itself in a kind of institutionalised nostalgia. John Relph, a man in his late 70s from New Jersey, said:

> We were raised to regard thrift, saving, frugality as essential to our future well-being. We were taught never to throw food away, to turn out the light when you left a room. We were careful with using the telephone and our house was always slightly underheated. It is amazing to see how indifferent people have become – it's almost as if they take delight in waste, in showing how little it matters that you use up things. I guess that reflects changes in society, but to us, the indifference of people never ceases to surprise, and in a disagreeable way. It is very irritating. You want to blame them, but of course it isn't their fault. They have been taught that generosity – what we could call squandering things – is more important than conserving them. People used to treasure the objects that belonged to their family, and expected to pass them on to a new generation. Now nothing lasts. Things perish and it is the people who go on and on.

In the 1970s, I developed a friendship with an elderly woman who was the widow of a former colonial official in Africa who had been knighted for his services to empire. For some reason, she had only a very small pension and lived in a hotel in Worthing, on the South Coast. She had one small room, which she had decorated with velvet drapes, pink lights and she perfumed it with incense sticks, which didn't quite cover the smell of sherry. She used to say, 'One hears so much about these angry young men. Well, I'm a furious old woman, but of course, no one has time for people like me.' She was characteristic of the returnees of empire who had come back to a world to which they could not adapt – egalitarian, pushy, hedonistic, colourful and uninhibited. She hated it and said she would have rather died in the bush than come back if she had known what awaited her. I would take her to lunch in a small restaurant where she complained loudly of the rudeness of the waitresses and the poor quality of the food. I felt the poignancy of what I took to be her desperate and lonely exclusion from life; and understood the pain of seeing the certainties of values and beliefs pass away, become relativised by time, a figure of fun to a new generation. I have found myself thinking of her more and more in recent years because it feels as though something similar has happened to me and to a generation of people who thought of themselves as socialists and grew up in the conviction of progress, the certainty of the better world and the inevitability, not only of economic but also social, and possibly even moral, improvement. How comic we look now to those who have grown to the wisdom of the market, to the knowledge of money and what it will buy, and how scorned and despised we are since we never knew what is now obvious to the whole world – that only the creation of wealth can raise up the people, only economic growth in perpetuity can bring hope to human kind. The kinship I felt with Lady Marling then was perhaps prescient; an intimation that even the most fixed beliefs can be swept away by time.

Today, economic and social change are taking place at a moment when more people than ever have reached old age. This leaves many old people disoriented and even embittered. There has always been tension between youth and age; but when the whole world has been caught up in violent discontinuities, associated with the end of socialism and the imposition of globalisation, the divide between the generations is bound to grow deeper. The sense of loss associated with ageing is exacerbated when the values, beliefs and certainties that underpin the social experience are suddenly removed. The socially marooned are a large, and increasing, proportion of elders in the world; and they are visible everywhere.

* * *

Lenin Sarani is a long, bleak thoroughfare of small metal-bashing units and repair workshops in Kolkata. On the crumbling pavement young men, covered with oil, dissect the engines of motorbikes with the precision of surgeons. Others are welding – fountains of blue and yellow sparks festive fireworks on the oil-stained sidewalk. Incongruously, churches from the Raj tower over these ramshackle structures – the Union Chapel, the Sacred Heart, the Methodist Chapel.

The Lawrence de Souza Home is a refuge for 30 Anglo-Indian widows and spinsters; set back from the road, it is a building of weather-beaten stone with stucco pillars, an upper-storey verandah and a compound shaded by mango, guava and neem trees.

In the spacious interior there is a plaque which reads: 'To the memory of Lawrence de Souza, died 30 October 1853, this asylum has been erected by his son, Lawrence Augustus de Souza, born on 5 April 1828, died in London on 27 April 1871 and buried at Dharamtallah Church in 1872.'

The residents know the story well and speak with a familiarity of Lawrence Augustus as though they had personally known their long dead benefactor. He shot and killed an Indian in a fight and was charged with murder. His mother made a vow that if her son were acquitted, she would crawl on her knees from Sealdah to Dharamtallah. He was found not guilty. At the point where his mother finished her expiatory pilgrimage, she built the church of the Sacred Heart. Lawrence later built the asylum nearby.

The building is comfortable. There are sofas and chairs around a long low table, with copies of *Reader's Digest*, newspapers and magazines, and a TV with a crucifix above it. In the afternoon, tea is served beneath the lofty pillars of the ornate open parlour, itself a kind of imperial sacrament in the chill of a Kolkata winter afternoon. Many of the women who live here bear the slightly archaic English names of their generation – Martha, Joyce, Sybil, Enid, Rhoda, Gloria.

They are among the more privileged Anglo-Indians. Most have worked, many in education. They are not bitter as many Anglo-Indians were after Independence. They exude a modest grace, a mixture of English gentility and Bengali *bhadralok*. Their position is poignant: the Calcutta in which they grew up no longer exists, and neither does the England of which they once dreamed.

Most no longer do so. Many had relatives who returned to Britain after Independence, and some of the women went to join them. They discovered that the values that they imagined governed life in Britain had long decayed. As young women, they had entertained fantasies that Britain was orderly, well mannered, 'civilised'. Their idealised view barely withstood the shock of contact; and they returned to an India that was, at least, familiar and comprehensible.

As old women, they now remember a Calcutta which sounds as unreal as the visions they had once of Britain, for theirs was a Calcutta of leisure and privilege. As children of professional families, their lives were comfortable, attended by a host of servants.

> Lunch always consisted of a side dish and a pudding. Dinner was formal. The cooks were mostly Muslim, very efficient, and they learned to prepare dishes that were half English – custards and pies and fried fish.

> In our colony, at three or four o'clock in the afternoon, everything was very still, as people took rest. The only sound was the chopping from every house, as the cooks prepared vegetables for the evening meal.

> We lived in the railway colony, which was almost entirely occupied by Anglo-Indian families. It was very pretty, bungalows among the gardens and flowers. In winter, we grew all the flowers of an English summer – dahlias and asters, salvias, antirrhinums, marigolds.

Many Anglo-Indians who had the means left at the time of Independence. 'They were so British, they couldn't tolerate the idea of Indian Raj. It meant their children would have to learn Bengali or Hindi, so they went for the sake of their children's future. Many were apprehensive about going. Until then, they had been nurses in hospitals, teachers, they worked in the telegraph office, the railways, in the fire brigade and police service.' Joyce remembers her boss with pride. 'Sir Richard Duckworth was a gentleman, but he lived life to the full. He owned tea estates, he lived in the grand style. I worked for his company for 50 years.'

Many went to England. Gloria joined her brother in Plymouth. She says sadly:

> I went for ever. I had no intention of coming back. But after one year teaching in a school there, I couldn't get home fast enough. In India, the children form a line. They are eager to learn. In England they just rushed around, they jumped in and out of the windows. When I tried to instil some discipline, one of the teachers said to me, 'We don't treat children like that any more.'

Joyce joined her family in Wales, but couldn't settle. She didn't like the food or the informality of social relationships. This unsettled her, as did the lack of respect for the elderly, the casual relationships between men and women, the breakdown of the family. Martha blames England for her diabetes and arthritis – the food and the climate – and was thankful to come back home, even though home itself bore little enough relation to what she had known as a child. 'Of course the countryside is very beautiful in summer. I admire the royal family. But we thought they were typical. We imagined they stood at the head of British society, a model and example to the people. This was not true. But the flowers and the gardens are lovely.' All say they have no 'longing' for England any more.

The Kolkata in which they have grown old, governed for the past quarter century by the Communist Party of India (Marxist), also presents to their wintry gaze an unfamiliar landscape, both physically and socially. They dwell elegiacally on the days when they went to the clubs in Park Street, to tea dances and parties; on the rickshaw-pullers harnessed between the long-handled shafts of elegant carriages, the clanging of the trams, the vast space of the Maidan, the horse races and Sunday promenades around the glistening confectionery architecture of the Victoria Memorial. They are sad that the authorities have neglected many of the most beautiful buildings. They have done this, they feel, out of ancient rancour against colonialism, and have allowed the ornate facades and overwrought structures to crumble, so that now shrubs and moss grow out of cracks in the masonry.

Many have known tragedy in their lives. Gloria's husband was killed in a motorbike accident in Delhi when he was only 42, and she had to bring up the children alone. Many of the children of the residents are now scattered – Gloria's daughter is a teacher in Dubai. Others have gone to Australia, the US. 'They say, "Come and live with us," but you can't uproot yourself all over again so late in life.'

Phyllis, 94, is the oldest resident. She is confined to bed and very deaf, but remains alert and takes a lively interest in the world. She worked in the Army and Navy Stores. Her father, a railwayman, was killed when he got down to inspect the line. Phyllis had only one daughter, whose photograph stands beside her bed. She was a sickly child who died aged 13. The sepia photo is faded, more than 60 years old. Phyllis says that her mother was told that she, Phyllis, would never survive. 'But here I am. I have outlived all my relatives.'

Women, they say, generally outlive their husbands. 'There are three reasons. One is that women liver longer than men. Second, men marry much younger women. And third, women are stronger than men anyway.' Mrs Jordan, who manages the home, says, 'If men had the first baby, there wouldn't be a second. Women know how to endure. Women don't give in. We hang on. That is our secret.'

During the daytime they are too busy to dwell too much on the past. 'Only at night-time we sometimes feel lonely and sad, when the thoughts return of those we have lost. When we were young, we dreamed of England. But now we have a lifetime of memories, and memories last longer than dreams.'

This experience is repeated all over the world: people uprooted, dislocated from the environment that formed them; migrants, refugees, the persecuted, the evictees of development and changing temper of the times. For some, it has been a slow exile, as the world around them changed and they didn't move. For others, it has been brutally disruptive: war, a change of regime, a natural catastrophe – the elderly, like the very young, suffer disproportionately. Both rich and poor are affected, intellectuals as well as workers and peasants.

I spoke to Professor Kweka, now in his 60s, professor of sociology at the University of Dar es Salaam.

> When I was young, I was trained as a primary schoolteacher. We lived at the mercy of colonial officers, whose job it was to give orders. It was ours to obey. I obeyed, and that is why I was promoted.
>
> With Independence, people felt they were free. Nyerere had a wide concept of freedom – unity, socialism and development. We felt that if we freed ourselves from the colonial yoke, we could also free ourselves from hunger, poverty and disease. Nyerere understood there was no point in governing or ruling if people died of hunger. So he instituted a system that answered basic needs, especially free education and free medical services. He saw the cultivation of human resources as the key to development. If the anxieties of life were reduced, if the old

were taken care of, the sick treated, the ignorant instructed, everything would be fine. Free water would be brought to the rural areas, there would be a nutrition programme, community health would take care of the worst diseases.

It had a dynamism and a purpose to which people responded. I grew up as a socialist and an idealist, not because of Nyerere, but as a Christian. My father was a Christian teacher, and my mother taught me the Bible. I looked at relationships among people, and realised at an early age that one person should not live above others to such a degree that it endangers their lives. In the same way, no country should leave another so far behind it creates anger and violence.

Nyerere said money doesn't bring development, because money is the weapon of the rich. Human beings are the real source of development.

The hopes were not fully realised. The real change occurred in 1986 when the International Monetary Fund and World Bank effectively took over. This brought about radical changes, 'cost-sharing' as it was called, but it meant people were charged for education and health care. This hurt the old and the vulnerable in particular.

It has been a bitter experience. It has changed the behaviour of people. When you are old, if your family do not take care of you – and many cannot, because of AIDS – you are on the streets. In consequence, corruption has become much worse. Of course, corruption has always existed, but before the mid-1980s, a corrupt person was regarded as unfortunate, selfish or greedy. Now it is normal.

The quality of life has deteriorated over the past 15 years, especially for the poor, the elderly, the sick, the AIDS orphans. Of course, society is not homogeneous. It has brought immense wealth to some people, but even the official figure of those in poverty is well over 50 per cent.

We have no room for manoeuvre, no room to decide for ourselves what we can do. We are more or less where we started – we have political power, but little of it remains in our hands. The situation has restored the status quo ante. This is why people talk of neo-colonialism. This hasn't created a new freedom struggle. Some people have said globalisation is a recipe for communist revolution. But in the meantime, it is a recipe for crime, stealing, robbery and killing others. Even travelling by bus has become dangerous. There have been bus hijacking. Gangs stop the bus and order the people to disembark. 'Give us everything you have.'

Was the vision of Nyerere given the opportunity to develop? The international community didn't appreciate Nyerere's ideas. It allowed – even encouraged – Tanzania to borrow money until it reached a state of bondage once more. Although there has been talk of writing off debts, the actual remission amounts to about 1 billion of a 7 billion dollar debt. This is just as crippling.

Of course, there were mistakes within. Nyerere spoke of basic education and health services, but that in itself was not enough. He talked of generating democracy from below, but he did not establish the machinery to achieve it. The people depended on ideas formulated from above. Nyerere insisted on the importance of planning, but the people were not in practice allowed to make plans of their own.

I've lived through these things and tried to transmit the values I believe in to my students. They are no longer preparing children for *ujamaa* but for the globalised environment. It seems that those in power think you can have development without self-reliance.

What parents tell their children is no longer meaningful. They say to an older generation, 'What do you know?' What the young know is money, and money is a poison to wisdom. The young have always revolted against the older generation, but now it is a more radical revolt, even though it is a conservative revolution, in the sense that they become the foot soldiers of global wealth and power.

They have destroyed hope in a better world. They have destroyed utopian ideals, and we, in our older years, must live among those ruins.

The migrants from South to North have noted – not always consciously, but with astonishment – that all the richness and diversity of the rural world they knew have been transformed into money.

Chloe, in her mid-60s, came to London from Jamaica in the mid-1950s. One of six children, she left the family landholding to work as a hospital cleaner. Her husband worked on the buses. In Hackney, she says, she learned new forms of poverty. At home, they had little money, but they were not resource-poor.

> You could go out and pick a fruit at any time. We grew vegetables and mangoes and pineapples. Everything you wanted for medicine was ready in the fields when you needed it. All you needed was the knowledge, what was good for headaches and fevers, sprains or diarrhoea, bleeding or sickness, and where to find them. Everything is still there, but people have forgotten. Everything they buy now comes from the US – big red apples, carrots, potatoes. Nothing is grown at home any more. That is poverty. And this is poverty here also, going down Ridley Road looking for cheap tomatoes or frozen chicken legs. At home we were free but didn't know it. Now we are not free there and we are not free here. The old people knew, but the youngsters don't want to know, because it is no use to them. They live in another world. You cannot tell them what you have seen. You are like someone who has lived on another planet, and they do not believe the stories you tell.

It is a common experience for migrants never really to accept that the site of their labour in exile will ever become their home; and they cherish an idea of the return, of retirement, of settling in old age in their home place. Visits over the years to family and neighbours fill them with longing; they are cherished and looked after, and they are sustained by the hope that this will, one day, become their life once more.

But going back is not so easy. Their own children have become anchored in the place of 'exile' and in any case, the values and mores of their home have also become unfamiliar.

> Dinesh came from Gujarat in India to London in 1966 when he was 23. He had a privileged posting with the Indian High Commission and was very excited at the prospect of living in Britain. From the beginning he was not particularly happy and lived in a series of uncomfortable bedsits in West London, where his life was constrained by what was then an overt racism. He wanted to go home but was told he would have to pay his own fare if he departed before the expiry of his contract. He remained, and met his future wife at work. She is handicapped by a profound deafness, but he loves her dearly,

and it seemed his future would be settled here. They had two children, and he found a job as a civil servant. The family remained somewhat isolated, and Dinesh sought to inculcate into his children a pious regard for their Hindu religion.

With time, things went wrong. Dinesh had carried with him certain notions of a middle-class Indian family, with himself as the head (he was the oldest of three brothers), the traditional paterfamilias, whose word was law. It soon became clear that the children were receiving instruction, both from school and from the media, which ran counter to what he was trying to convey to them. The son quarrelled and left home. He married a woman several years older than he was, a relationship to which his parents did not consent. The daughter left university, married a British man, who became the house-husband while she worked. The idea Dinesh had of his daughter's marriage was that she should be given, submissive and adored by her father, to a groom chosen by her parents.

This double estrangement led to Dinesh's deep depression and nervous collapse. He took early retirement from work. He went back to India for a time, where his extended family offered some consolation and reaffirmed his status as head of the family. He recovered. In his mid-50s, the only work he could find he thought demeaning – dispatch clerk for a fast-food outfit, 'junior' clerk in a university department. He accumulated three or four files of letters of application for jobs, to the majority of which he received no reply. He says simply, 'I have lost everything – my job, my family, my life. I might as well dig my own grave.' Dinesh's loss of status and diminution of self-respect were made even more extreme by the cultural limbo in which he spent so many years, where he had preserved older attitudes of his culture of origin, shielded by isolation from the country into which he had migrated. His discovery on returning to India was that society there had not stood still either, and he no longer received the recognition or status that he might once have enjoyed.

POVERTY IN OLD AGE

Most people in the world who live to be old are poor; and labour is their major source of survival. In societies where there is no expectation of comfort in old age, and the best that can be expected is to be fed and sheltered, this is a less terrible prospect than it is in affluent societies. Indeed, historically, this was probably the experience of a majority in Europe. Death was such a familiar companion of pre-industrial life in Europe that family 'stability' is an illusion. In eighteenth-century France, out of every 100 children, only 20 would reach the age of 50, and only ten the age of 70. Death affected all age groups and was not solely a visitation upon the old. Almost 30 per cent of children died before the age of 15. Security, in these conditions was, at best, only provisional, and even then, often threatened by hunger and insufficiency.[11]

In Western Europe today, where the majority of elderly are not poor, those who remain in poverty are doubly estranged from society. Participation becomes problematical, particularly when this is focused so intensely upon *buying in* all that is necessary for a good or even adequate life. 'Social exclusion' becomes synonymous with economic exclusion, when to spend is to participate. Many older people who were brought up to thrift and self-restraint are shocked by what they see as the wastefulness that has become the norm. To seek to answer 'basic needs' in a culture the purpose of which has ceased to revolve around any such thing is at best a poor makeshift, a perfunctory humanitarian gesture that nevertheless leaves the elderly poor on the outside of the steadily rising income which the majority now expect.

* * *

The inner city means not only ethnic minorities and transients, but also poor older people. It also means sub-standard housing, privately rented flats, dilapidation and an exclusion made the worse by virtue of the fact that the elderly live among a younger and more vigorous population, which only emphasises their sense of isolation. One old woman in South London said to me, 'Old age is another country. And so is where I live. I feel I've gone abroad and I never went anywhere.' She was not being racist.

The inner city means short-life housing, downmarket shops where you can buy damaged tinned goods, past the sell-by-date food, inferior produce. It is a diet of toasted white bread, margarine, jam and tea, slices of ham and eggs, tinned meat and soup. It is a draughty place, with paper or rags blocking the windows where the sashes have rotted, where condensation silvers the windows and the water runs in crooked fingers down the pane; of kitchens where people sit to keep warm by the heat of the oven. Old women sit in chunky cardigans in greasy armchairs, while the gas fire hisses, and they read yesterday's newspaper that somebody left behind on the bus. The wind rattles through the streets and gets stuck in the chimneys, and the dogs scavenge around the dustbins, while the waste paper and empty fast-food containers blow against the legs in the bus shelter with its splintered glass and the menacing graffiti.

The inner city is also a place of fear and insecurity; where the only new things in the flat are the safety chain behind the door, from the time when the old woman came home to find the wood split and the door shattered and the clock that had stood in her mother's house and the few pounds in the teapot had gone. It is rumoured that the hot meal twice a week at the centre is going to be cut to one day a week. Even the trip to Bingo on Thursday nights has become stressful, the bus doesn't come and if there is a gang of kids getting on you wait for the next one because you are never sure whether the reason why they are talking so loudly and fooling about is because they are on drugs.

The inner city is loneliness and indifference. It is the place where you monitor your own decline of sleep, waking up in what you think is the early morning, but the luminous hands of the metal clock by the bed tell you it is only twelve thirty. It is the long wait in the doctor's surgery, the request for sleeping tablets, or something for your nerves, this anxiety that is your constant companion. Will the familiar doctor be on duty, or will you be passed to someone you can't even begin to explain to all over again the dizzy spells and the dry mouth and the pervasive feeling of ill being. It is also, as a woman in her late 70s said, 'being used to nothing in life and not being disappointed at what you've never had'. It is stoicism and boredom, endurance, waiting for the telephone call from the son, the visit from the grandchildren, and you wonder what little treat you can afford for them that will make them smile. It is television throughout the day for company, the sunlight falling on the screen, fading the picture and showing up the dust you no longer have the heart to get up and brush away. It is not drinking after five o'clock so you don't have to get up in the night in the cold lavatory with the frosted glass. It is no longer being able to bathe until the daughter comes to help you in and out, in spite of the handrails. It is a dread that the place smells, not of dirt, but of old age, the faint musty smell of continuous habitation, the exhalations of age and the window that doesn't open even in summer. It is above all the time of waiting, waiting for change that can only mean loss.

The familiar house is now a place of great danger; the cuff striking the saucepan with the single egg in boiling water, the frayed edge of the carpet, the stairs you no longer even try to go up, the bed in the living room that demonstrates to you constantly your growing immobility. You fear sickness in the night, even though you have the button at your wrist that will summon the agency you should have a fall. But what if it is sudden, what if I fall unconscious? If the neighbours even notice you and smile, you feel a pleasure quite out of proportion to the small social contact. You don't even want to go and have a cup of tea with the woman next door because she only repeats the same things and if you hear one more word about her children, while she listens to nothing you say, you'll scream... Sometimes you remember, the children, the husband who died within three months of retirement, and above all the tenderness of your own parents, and you feel unloved, especially since the cat died and you couldn't bear to replace him, and anyway, although you never said it to yourself, he would probably outlive you. You know the children would come in an emergency, but you don't want to trouble them, and you try to resist lifting the phone because that will only worry them, and in any case, you may need them soon enough in a real emergency...

The circumstances of poverty in old age vary widely, but the sentiments that attend it transcend the incidental details of this or that climate, culture or custom. People are always old and poor in the same way.

OLD AGE AND TRAUMATIC SOCIAL CIRCUMSTANCES

In parts of the world, older people are stranded in harsher ways by the passing of regimes and social systems that afforded them some protection. The story of steadily increasing life expectancy does not apply to what are sometimes euphemistically referred to as the 'transitional economies' of Eastern Europe. Where welfare systems have been dismantled, the elderly make up a large proportion of the victims of the 'shock therapy', whereby a market economy was rapidly imposed on a decayed and bankrupt socialism. In the Russian Federation between 1987 and 1994, life expectancy fell: the precise figure is contested, but there was a surplus of deaths over births approaching three quarters of a million as recently as 1998. This was due, in part, to rising abuse of alcohol and drugs which came in the wake of increased poverty and insecurity.

Some demographers have estimated that the population of Russia could halve in the next 20 years, and the number of pensioners could equal the number of workers.[12] Whatever the iniquities of Communism – and these require no further rehearsing – the cancellation of an ideology in which people have lived – however alienated they may have been – leaves them with a sense, not of liberation but of meaninglessness. Even if the official ideology of the state did not gain their acceptance, the values it represented were an integral part of their life. They had made their accommodation with it. It is, perhaps, in this area that we should look if we want to understand the upsurge of sickness, the loss of faith in the future, the self-harm people do themselves with drugs and alcohol. This is recognised to some degree. In *Policy Review*, Nicholas Eberstadt stated, 'Although the USSR's departure from the world stage was remarkably peaceful, the collapse of the Soviet system nevertheless brought on a veritable explosion of mortality in Russia. Between 1989–91 and 1994, crude death rates in Russia shot up by 40 per cent.'[13] He says that the 'excess mortality' of Russia between 1992 and 98 is likely to exceed 3 million deaths – equivalent to the casualties of a significant war. Although a proportion of these deaths can be ascribed to alcoholism and violent crime among young men, Eberstadt goes on to say, 'Russian men in their 40s and 50s are dying at a pace that may never have been witnessed during peacetime in a society distinguished by urbanisation and mass education.' Among these, heart disease is the major cause of death, followed by 'injuries' – including suicide, murder and poisonings. In 1996, for instance, 35,000 Russians died from accidental alcohol poisoning.

The death rates tell little about the chronic sickness, depression and loss of purpose that may cause suffering to those of an older generation without killing them. When societies collapse, people die of grief: the fate of the Aboriginals of Australia and the indigenous peoples of both North and South America supply plenty of examples. Once the system of belief that underpins a society is weakened, and people lose faith in it, they are susceptible to forms of despair and experiences of loss usually associated with bereavement.

A loss of coherence and meaning come in the wake of such catastrophes. It is true that in the 1980s the Soviet Union had a higher ratio of hospital beds to population than any other country in the world. Its structure of care for the elderly was comprehensive. Although the imposition of the market, falling investment in health care, bribery and demoralisation of staff contribute to accelerating death rates, the social pathology associated with the loss of faith may well prove to have been a more important factor. It is scarcely surprising that a majority of members of the Communist Party in post-Soviet Russia are elderly. TV images of demonstrations by the Party in Moscow or St Petersburg against the market are often derided for their adherence to an archaic and discredited system. But the loss of value in pensions, the breakdown in health care, the marginalisation and exclusion are exacerbated by a profound psychological injury to their sense of identity. It is perhaps asking too much for the victorious of the Cold War to extend much sympathy to those on the losing side, even though many of the elders of Russia had lived through some of the most momentous and tragic events the world has witnessed during the twentieth century. To mock them, in their padded coats and mittens, clumsy boots stamping against the cold as 'the old guard', the 'party faithful', the unreconstructed of a defunct Communism is only one symptom of the triumphalism, not merely of one ideology over another, but also of the young over the old.

The United Nations Population Division projects that male life expectancy in Russia in 2010–15 will be barely higher than it was in the early 1960s.

* * *

In other parts of Europe, disruption to life and livelihood has been more severe. In Serbia, for example, by the late 1990s, the over-60s constituted 17 per cent of the population. This reflects the movement of many older Serbs displaced from other parts of the former Federal Republic of Yugoslavia.[14] The value of pensions and savings of older Serbs fell dramatically, and mass unemployment eroded the capacity of younger people to support the elderly. This has imposed new responsibilities upon the elderly themselves, both to contribute to family income and to take care of their own health and well-being just as they are at their most vulnerable. The conflicts of 1991–95, and the redrawing of boundaries, led to an exodus of people from Bosnia-Herzegovina and Croatia, while many others were displaced by the violence in Kosovo. Many still live in collective refuges or in rented accommodation.

The material deficiencies of many older refugees are obvious; we must add to this the psychological disorientation that comes from the disintegration of society and the ideology which held it together, within which people had developed their own strategies for coping. Of the 100,000 refugees still housed in collective centres, one-third are older people. Their political and legal status remains undefined while their pensions and property are inaccessible. There is widespread apprehension in Serbia among the elderly, especially in the refugee camps, over their chances to lead a secure and settled life in their declining years.

Comprehensive state provision for social security existed in the former Yugoslavia. It has been ruined by 'economic transition', the subsequent crisis in public funding and the costs of war. In theory, state pensions for the elderly remain a universal entitlement, but the level of payment no longer covers basic needs – food, rent and heating in winter. In any case, payment of pensions has been disrupted by war, and where international agencies offered food aid, stories of this being sold are widespread in order to maintain rent payments. One in five older Serbs is without any family support.

Health care, too, technically free for the over-65s, has been undermined by the crisis in funding. This had a disproportionate effect on the elderly – a combination of poor nutrition and high levels of stress led to a sharp rise in mortality rates during the 1990s. Staff shortages in health centres and hospitals, and an interruption in the supply of drugs, have forced those who can to use private clinics. The majority simply go untreated.

The family tradition of caring for the elderly saves many from destitution, but some families are no longer in a position to do so. Many old people living alone are very isolated. Residential care is limited and inadequate. There is little prospect that the elderly will receive the community-based small-scale care which would be both the most effective and least expensive support they need.

Older people are simply not seen as a priority given all the other urgent demands on resources. The forced removals by conflict have also disrupted the traditional survival practices of all agrarian peoples – growing vegetables and fruit for consumption, gathering fuel, keeping chickens, animal husbandry.

Some older people are working voluntarily, offering time, experience and ideas in the formation of self-help groups and associations, but the sheer pressure of surviving makes this extremely difficult.

HelpAge International reported that people living in the collective centres have minimal amenities. These are often in remote places and conditions remain unhygienic. 'At one centre, older people had the right to emergency treatment in hospital, but first had to get a written referral from the doctor, 3 kilometres away. They had no money for bus fares, and little contact with anyone outside the centre who could help.' People said they felt isolated and invisible. Their presence in the community was often resented. More than 200 older people in collective centres committed suicide in one year.

This testimony, gathered by HelpAge International, is characteristic.

> I'm 65 and I come from Croatia, where I lived on a farm. We had a good life there – we kept sheep, cows and pigs. We were always busy. We left Croatia six years ago, during Operation Storm, with all of us – my husband and two daughters, and me – perched on a tractor. My youngest daughter, aged 20, drove. Her husband was away fighting. But we lost the tractor and all the things we had with us on the journey, and had to come part of the way on foot. At one point, we were taken prisoner.

We spent our first year in Serbia with my husband's brother. Then my husband managed to get us a room here in the collective centre. To begin with, there were five people to a room. We had no bed, but we asked the Yugoslav Red Cross for help and we got a sponge mattress. We have been here five years now. We are used to it, though we still feel sad a lot of the time, and my husband especially cannot forget the past. We have a garden we can work in, but it's not good soil like our farm used to be.

We haven't any pension here. We would have had one in Croatia. Luckily, my husband got a temporary job with the city parks, and my daughters have the odd bit of work. But I worry about money. Both of us have high blood pressure and a heart condition.

Now we have nothing left. My husband and one of my daughters went back once more to see what was left of our home, and there was nothing of ours any more. Everything was burned down, because our village was near some military installations that got bombed during the war. Some people have gone back to the villages, but our village has gone.[15]

When the very places where people have lived are wiped out, this negates their whole life and is itself a form of bereavement.

The death rate among elderly refugees is high. Among the estimated 6,500,000 refugees in Africa, it is the very young and the very old who die first.

In Rwanda, despite the negative impact such programmes have had elsewhere, a forced villagisation programme has been in place since late 1996, whereby people have been displaced and resettled in *imidugudu*, officially designated villages. Many people have been forced to destroy their homes before moving; others have had land confiscated for construction sites. Those refusing to move have been subject to arrest, harassment and imprisonment.

Without consultation or participation of any kind, this policy was announced after the 1994 genocide, when resettlement programmes were urgently needed, and international donors were contributing to the costs of restabilising refugees and the survivors of the massacres. What was originally an emergency issue, with the return of almost 4 million refugees within three years, became a government forced relocation policy.

Many *imidugudu* are occupied mainly by poor and vulnerable people and, according to non-governmental organisations, they are places where the sickly and old go to die. The provision of shelter has been given priority, with little attention to running water, schools, health centres. The rationale for this, according to the government of Rwanda, is 'for the purpose of proper land utilisation and the provision of basic services. The programme seeks to establish commercial activities and employment outside the agricultural sector.'[16]

A report from Human Rights Watch in 2001 notes that a substantial number of heads of household in *imidugudu* are drawn from the most vulnerable sectors of society. According to one survey, 59 per cent were women, 5 per cent were under the age of 20, and 7 per cent were over 60. Among them were widows, who feared for their security and welcomed the chance to live in a group.

The report states:

> The elderly also suffer greatly from having to move. Seven of twelve persons who had to destroy their homes in one cell of Ruhengeri commune were over the age of sixty, and one was an eighty-year-old woman. Half the cultivators who had their crops destroyed when land was cleared from a building site in another cell of the same commune were over the age of sixty.
>
> In some cases local officials organized other residents to help the weak and elderly. In others religious or humanitarian organizations mustered workers to help build houses. But given the scarcity of resources for most of the *imidugudu*, the neediest could not rely on help being either abundant or long-term.

During emergencies, famines, war, natural disasters, the elderly suffer disproportionately. The less mobile cannot even become refugees; left behind in war zones, they face bombardment and, as occurred in Kosovo, vengeful harassment. The images from Chechnya, of elderly women emerging from fetid basements and cellars to pick their way through the rubble of Grozny in search of basic provisions, remain an enduring symbol of their fate. Sometimes, survival itself can become a burden to the very old: those who came out of the Nazi extermination camps, who survived the genocidal frenzy in Rwanda, who experienced the massacres of the Liberation War in Bangladesh, are haunted by traumas *which no one else remembers*.

> Amina Begum is in her 70s; an upright, dignified woman in a dark green saree. She lives with her son and his wife in Barisal, in the south of Bangladesh, in a modest tin-set house. Her husband and older son were killed during the war of 1971 which brought Bangladesh into existence. She keeps their photograph on a wooden shelf covered, incongruously, with a length of faded Christmas paper decorated with bells and holly. Her younger son is a construction worker. Their house stands on what remains of family land, half of which was claimed by the river, the rest sold to pay for survival when her son was young. Amina says, looking at the photograph, 'I wish I could have died in their place. My son was 18. It is the worst thing that can happen to a mother, to see her son die before her. He will always remain 18. I have grown old, but he is still 18. My husband, too, was a strong man. His hair will never turn white, I see him still as he went off to fight the Pakistani army for the freedom of our Bengal. He was betrayed by the *rajaker* (collaborators). They waited to ambush them as they swam across the river. My life goes on uselessly. My only consolation is that every day brings me closer to my husband and my son.'

Jennifer Inger has worked with the Red Cross in Bosnia-Herzegovina, where a programme of home visiting to 15,000 vulnerable elderly in Sarajevo proved to be, literally, a life-saving operation. 'There is no normal community support. Families are dead, or have fled; the government cannot provide even the most elementary services.' A thousand volunteers, many of them elderly, have also initiated cross-community contacts. In these cases, the elderly have become agents of reconciliation between the Serb, Croat and Muslim communities. 'There is no chance that government services can be restored in the near future. The position of the elderly has also mobilised the more active pensioners, who have been on marches, blocked the roads. The Red Cross is the biggest provider of social services in the country.'

It seems that the rhetoric of 'giving' the elderly a purpose, integrating them into society, remains largely theoretical until harsh material circumstances fall forth their otherwise neglected energies. This is a sobering prospect for the industrialised countries, pondering on how to activate the dormant powers of their ageing peoples. Can a role be found for them without a major disaster? Or, in order to prolong economic life, will a whole new generation, now young, have to be made poor?

Chapter 4

AN AGEING WORLD: RELATIONS BETWEEN NORTH AND SOUTH

Whenever people from other cultures criticise the West, it is not long before the issue of the treatment of the elderly arises. In November 2001, the Organisation of African Unity called a conference in Nairobi on the ageing of the population of the continent. The number of people in Africa over 60 is expected to grow from 38 million today to 212 million by 2050. A characteristic comment was picked up by the BBC:

> We have our extended families. This is the backbone of our societies, I know many in the West do not understand what a family is, what relatives are in the true sense, but the family is a treasure. They are not a financial burden, as not everything has a price. It is because of this that Africa will pull through, that nations will pull through. It is colonialism that attempted to destroy the culture. The old still have authority, they are patriarchs. (Bhekuzulu Khumalo, *Talking Point*, November 29, 2001)

A retired army officer in India said to me in September 2000:

> The Indian family is indestructible. The members of the family are exactly what the word says – they are members, like the limbs of the same body. We do not follow the individualism of the West. The survival of the family group is what matters. This is deep in our culture, and it has withstood the assaults of imperialism and neo-colonialism. It will save us from the excesses of your country, the neglect of the elderly. I am 70 years old. My son and daughter-in-law live with my family and that of my brother. We may have differences, even quarrels, but the family is the institution that ensures order and continuity. I am its head, and my son will follow me in due course. That is why my authority is complete – every judgement I make is designed to ensure the stability of the family. I have fought for my country in two wars against

> Pakistan, and at the same time I was fighting for the preservation of my family.

Such statements represent a kind of heroic defiance in the presence of the forces of dissolution of traditional patterns of living in the world. The question to ask those who see their culture as a defensive bulwark against the onslaught of globalisation is whether they think the alleged Western indifference to the family is an inherent part of Western culture. They mistake the nature of 'development' which has loosened – but not broken – the bonds of kinship in the West. This 'development' is now being exported worldwide. How did it happen that in the West many primary long-term carers of the aged and vulnerable are now strangers, paid functionaries – home care workers, care assistants, social workers, geriatric medical personnel, nursing auxiliaries, the objects of the labour of others? What transformed the enfeeblement of age into the raw material for strange new economic specialisms in the division of labour that has called into existence the mysteriously named 'caring professions'?

First of all, it is not the cold-heartedness of the people of the West that has brought about this state of affairs. Nor is it true that the West has 'abandoned' its elderly. The great majority of older people are in close and constant touch with their families, and turn to them for support and succour when they are in need. The improved health of the elderly has enabled many to continue to live independently, even after the loss of a spouse. What is true is that the daily proximity of kinsfolk and the constant attendance have diminished. The weakening of the ties of kinship rarely manifests itself in the 'abandonment' of the elderly. Certainly, there is greater loneliness, loved ones may not devote the same time to old people, and it is true that in Britain almost half a million elderly people live in residential and nursing homes. Almost one in three households in Britain and the US now consist of a single person, the great majority of them widows or widowers. But any weakening of the obligations of kinship derives not from callousness but from economic necessity.

Globalisation will certainly see an intensification of the developments that have led to this. Increased migrations, the uprooting of whole peoples, the long march of humanity in search of a 'better life' have scattered populations in pursuit of self-improvement. We lived through this in Britain at an earlier stage of industrialisation when people first forsook fields and villages to settle in factory and mill towns, in tenements and back-to-back slums of the great cities. At that time, villages were abandoned, people migrated to an unfamiliar environment, leaving only the old to remember and to mourn, much as is happening in Asia and Africa today. Within the past few years more than half the world's population have become urban-dwellers. Oliver Goldsmith, in 'The Deserted Village', evoked the experience almost two and a half centuries ago:

> But now the sounds of population fail,
> No cheerful murmurs fluctuate in the gale,
> No busy steps the grass-grown footway tread,
> For all the bloomy blush of life is fled!
> All but yon widow'd solitary thing
> That feebly bends beside the plashy spring:
> She, wretched matron, forc'd in age for bread
> To strip the brook with mantling cresses spread,
> To pick her wintry faggot from the thorn,
> To seek her nightly shed, and weep till morn;
> She only left of all the harmless train,
> The sad historian of the pensive plain.

How this prefigures the image of villages in parts of the north of Thailand, in Andhra Pradesh, in Bangladesh, and, for other reasons, in Tanzania and many other countries of South and East Africa! The similarities are veiled only by a different landscape, another colour of flesh, a different climate. The compulsions that tore up an ancient peasantry from the earth of Britain are at work worldwide. They oblige the young and able to leave behind the old and weak as they move to seek work in factories, on construction sites, in transport, as domestic servants, as vendors, drivers and security guards. In Britain, the departure of the able-bodied young forced many elderly to seek parish relief, or to take refuge in the gloomy shelter of the workhouse.

Even so, it remained the concern of the vast majority of families that they should continue to look after those left behind, the elderly and bereft. There was no less love between the generations than there is in the South today. But in spite of that, families *were* torn apart, by sickness, premature death, by migration and especially by emigration – millions of people left Britain, many of them driven by unemployment or the hope of making a better life in the lands of imperial conquest. These departures were no less reluctant or full of apprehension than they are in the poor world today; indeed, they were often more irreversible, since few had the resources to return to their homelands once the decision to depart had been taken. Many knew that the separations on the quays of Liverpool or the docks at Tilbury would be their last meeting in life.

Not should it be imagined today that the people of the West consign their loved ones to the ministrations of ill-paid functionaries of the state or to nursing homes casually. When they do so, it is under duress, as a result of inescapable pressure, and when all other choices have been exhausted. And, as we have seen, many people continue to sacrifice themselves to look after the very old when they themselves are retired. The social costs to Western society, which many in the South deplore, are not a consequence of the unkindness or insentience of the people but of lack of choice.

Given the spread of this model of development worldwide, it would be surprising if some of the dilemmas of people in the rich world did not begin to show themselves in countries where the family remains a source of much self-congratulation. Many non-resident Indians pay out considerable sums for their parents to be cared for by servants and carers, as well as in homes that are beginning to appear all over the sub-continent. It is, not surprisingly, the more privileged and highly educated classes who are the first to face these troubling decisions.

Rajiv, an information technology worker in Dallas, says,

> We wanted to bring my mother to the States. She wouldn't leave India. She gave all kinds of reasons. She didn't like the fact that there are no servants in America. She has always been used to having someone cook for her, do the shopping, clean and wash the house, and she has her own driver. When she came to stay with us, it used to make her angry that we left all the dirty dishes in the sink overnight. She had always had someone to do everything for her. Then she wouldn't leave the place where she had lived with her family for 40 years. She didn't want to leave the spirit of those who had died there.

> What to do? We provided her with servants, but she thought they were stealing from her. Our lives are here now, and our children have been raised here – they can't go back to India. So we are caught between cultures, and my mother's refusal to change tears us in two.

All over the world, people are learning that whether or not they take care of their elderly is less a question of family commitment than a question of economics. An increasingly complex global division of labour is taking individuals across the world in search of livelihood. On the one hand, those with expertise and qualifications gravitate towards the places where they will command the highest salaries; on the other, the degradation of rural life compels poor people into seasonal, contractual or permanent migration. In both cases, those *left behind* suffer most; and to be old is, increasingly, to be among the left behind in every sense.

Close to the hotel where I sometimes stay in Dhaka, there is an abandoned two-storied villa dating from the time when Bangladesh was still East Pakistan. It has been invaded by scores of families. The building is peeling and derelict, the ornamental concrete crumbling. In each room two or three families have made a kind of home. The courtyard is also occupied by squatters, while outside the compound wall, rough shelters have also been constructed, hessian and polythene tied with string to the balustrade, and weighed down by stones in the gutter. These are the lodgings of construction workers from the north of Bangladesh. Sharina lives here with her husband and her daughter, Jehanara. Jehanara was run over by a car, and both her legs are encased in grubby plaster. Sharina says they left their village near Dinajpur, as many others have done, to work on one of the building sites that are such a conspicuous part of the city landscape. They left their elderly parents.

> In our village, when we are away there is no one to look after our families. We send money home so they will not be hungry. When they need medicine we send a little more. But if something serious happens, we can do nothing. My mother was bitten by a snake in the monsoon and she almost died. We love our parents of course, but we cannot bring them to live on the street. We are construction workers, and we have nowhere to stay but the street. You cannot bring old people to such

> dangerous places. My mother is very old. She must be 50. We are landless people, with only a small homestead in the village. My mother tells me the village is a village of ghosts because only the very old remain there.

In the cities of South Asia, the tearing apart of flesh and blood is almost audible as sons and daughters make their involuntary departure from village and farmstead. It would be as mistaken to attribute these 'abandonments' to hard-heartedness as it would to blame the people of the West for failing to live with their parents or 'putting them into a home'. Such actions are part of a necessity which it becomes more difficult to opt out of. 'Of course you must go' or 'You have your own life to lead', parents say to their children, indicating that they recognise that there is no remedy for what might appear, superficially, to be the desertion of those who nurtured them. In this way, emotions of people in the favoured places of the world vary little from those in the most wretched sites of exploitation and poverty.

THE UNITED STATES

The United States, where the issue of ageing is nowhere near as acute as in Europe, nevertheless recognises that even with a projected 20 per cent of over-65s by 2050, the elderly population will double. Life expectancy in the United States stood at 47 in 1900, reached 68 in 1950, and rose to 76 in 1991 (79 for women, 72 for men). An American who reaches 65 can expect to live another 17 years. California has the highest absolute number of elderly (3.3 million), while Florida has the highest proportion of over-65s – 19 per cent.

In 1992, about three in four persons between 65 and 74 considered their health to be good. Two in three aged 75 and over also said they were in good health. While 1 per cent of those aged 65–74 lived in a nursing home, one in four of those over 85 did. Fifty per cent of people aged 85 or older needed assistance performing everyday activities such as bathing, moving around at home and preparing meals. In the coming decades, there will be more people in their 50s and 60s caring for very elderly and frail dependants (Source: Census Bureau of US).

The US, operating at close to full employment, has seen a big increase in the employment of those beyond the retirement age. The US, together with such diverse countries as Australia, the Czech Republic, Germany, Hungary and Sweden, has announced plans to raise the state pension age.

In the US, a long-term trend to earlier retirement has been reversed since the mid-1980s. The International Longevity Center in New York released a report in 2001 by Kenneth Knapp and Charlotte Muller revealing that people over 65 are particularly well represented in four areas of economic activity: independent contractors (such as accountants); on-call workers (such as substitute teachers); temporary workers (for example, receptionists filling in for sick employees); and workers provided by contract firms (such as computer programmers working in the office of a customer). The authors conclude that, contrary to all expectations, no other age group shows such a strong propensity to work in non-traditional employment.

The US is faced with no immediate crisis of an ageing population, partly because of continuing migration. According to the census of 2002, 11 per cent of the population of the US were born outside the country. By European standards, the estimated proportion of the elderly seems more than manageable; but the idea of a sclerosis of the population has begun to disturb many of the elite of what likes to think of itself as 'a young country', a place of endless dynamism and innovation.

The arguments are starkly presented. On one side, there are those like Paul Hewitt, of the Center for Strategic and International Studies, who claim that the ageing population of the world could lead to a new era of instability and insecurity worldwide. By 2030, about 30 countries are expected to have falling populations. In the West, Hewitt predicts this will lead to 'fiscal meltdown', with labour shortages, falling rates of saving and declining asset values. Against this, people such as Victor Marshall, director of the University of North Carolina Institute on Aging, believes that improvements in health care will ensure that economic activity will continue into old age, and that a judicious blending of the capacities of young and old will ease the transition to a lower population in the world, which in turn will ease pressure on resources and the global environment. Workforce participation will rise, productivity increase; the ageing of the world should be seen as an achievement of civilisation, a symbol of success rather than a catastrophe. Ageing is one of the greatest triumphs of the contemporary world.

Hewitt's argument is made more compelling by the fear that ageing, and the diversion of resources from defence spending to care of the elderly, may result in problems regarding the ability of the US to maintain its military supremacy. It is possible that leadership of the world may pass to more dynamic countries. An article in the *New York Herald Tribune* (January 30, 2001) suggested that 'hordes of grey-haired retirees could ultimately do more damage to globalisation than the youthful activists who these days often try to disturb international economic meetings'. In the presence of an ageing population, other, more thrusting, energetic and youthful Third World countries might oust the United States from its position of supremacy in the world.

This, then is the bottom line: the hegemony of the US is menaced by the elderly, as more money is absorbed by attending to their well-being, and society loses its productivity gains and becomes less inventive, less enterprising, less capable of self-renewal. This anxiety lends the issue great significance in the think tanks and universities of the US, of the IMF and World Bank and the OECD. Hewitt says, 'It is no good looking to immigration as a panacea. To maintain today's ratio of active workers to retirees solely through immigration would require far more immigrants than would be politically acceptable either in Europe or the United States.'

It seems that the optimistic version of the future is for official consumption. If the most respected agencies and institutions in the United States regard the ageing population as even a remote threat to its power, we should take it very seriously indeed.

(This helps, perhaps, to explain certain contradictions in Britain's response to its own possible demographic crisis. For while publicly mounting a display of formal evictions of asylum seekers, the government has also been busy with its 'fast-track' access to Britain for skilled workers. With the rise of right-wing populism all over Europe, and local successes for the British National Party, governments are anxious not to be seen as 'soft' on migrants. But the tax base, the social security system, the public services require more and younger workers. No government has seen fit to debate these issues with the people.

The migrants, the foreigners, the seekers of asylum, those who might be seen as potential carers, the sustainers of the elderly, are perceived by them as a threat to their well-being. It is a supreme irony that many such people come from societies where older networks of protection of the weak and the elderly have not been broken. When they are seen as aliens, or worse as criminals, a threat to the very 'security' they might provide for the elderly, how will they employ their capacity for caring in a country which rejects them with such superficial and uncharitable unconcern?

It seems the government is rejuvenating the population by stealth. For without such a renewal, perhaps the next generation really will have to work into their 70s in order to continue contributing to the diminished pensions they must expect. With time, instead of crusades against child workers in the world, we shall perhaps witness the rise of campaigns against geriatric labour, and not in the dark places of Asia and Africa, but in the heart of Europe. People will be moved by the scandal of arthritic fingers and failing eyesight, as workers seek to increase productivity in the export-processing zones of the France or Germany of the future. Maybe, behind the tills of fast-food outlets, the have-a-nice-day culture will be serviced by the rheumy eyes and varicose veins of the unretired.)

CHINA

State intervention in population control has been at its most extreme in China. Since 1979 the 'one-child policy' has imposed severe penalties on families which have more than one, or at most two, children. This, together with market-driven reforms, has had unforeseen consequences. By the standards of developing countries, the proportion of people over 60 is high – more than 10 per cent. There are 8 million people over 80, a number growing by 5.4 per cent annually.

Prenatal scans are now available in towns and even villages all over China. Many recent studies suggest that many people are aborting girl-children, to ensure that the limits on family size will provide them with a son – a more certain guarantor of help in their old age since girls move away from their parents' home when they marry. In certain parts of the countryside, according to the *New York Times* (June 22, 2002), there are as many as 144 boys for every 100 girls. This is exacerbated by the breakdown even of any pretence that the socialist system can provide a social security or medical care system, especially in the villages. The imbalance is less pronounced in some of the poor and remote areas, especially in Tibet and in the Muslim region of Xinjiang.

The 1990 census found a national imbalance of 110 boys for every 100 girls. By 2000, this had reached 117. (The international average is about 106 boys for every 100 girls.) Significantly, the greatest distortions were recorded in two of the most prosperous south-eastern provinces. A similar tendency is present in India, South Korea and Taiwan – all cultures where brides go to the family home of the male. The ready availability of ultrasound scans mixes high technology with traditional social values, so that conservatism becomes regressive and deeply damaging to women.

These developments in China, together with the growing numbers of the elderly, will have profound and unpredictable effects upon society. It may be that young couples will become responsible for four parents and eight grandparents, and with growing longevity, some surviving great-grandparents too. The absence of a social safety net, even with a modest 10 per cent of over-60s, is unlikely to be remedied in the near future; and as the percentage doubles within two generations, it is doubtful whether the rising income even from China's successful market economy will meet the growing costs of care.

The effect of the high proportion of elderly on the supply of labour is likely to be severe. By 2000, according to Zhang Benbo, a researcher with the State Planning Commission, 24 per cent of the active labour force was 45 or older; by 2040, this is expected to rise to 37 per cent.

In 1978 there was one retired person in China for every 30.3 workers. In 1999, the ratio was one retired person for every 3.7 employees. If the current retirement age remains unchanged (at 55 for women and 60 for men), the ratio may be one retired person for every 2.4 employees by 2030 – virtually identical to that of Britain.

John Gittings, reporting from Shanghai for the *Guardian* on October 22, 2001, wrote that life expectancy in China as a whole is now 71, and that in the city of Shanghai, 18 per cent of the people are over 60. This proportion is expected to double in the next 20 years. A survey in Shanghai in 2000 revealed that one in four of the city's elderly people suffered from depression. This is, perhaps, not surprising. The fabric of the city has been transformed in the last 20 years. Apartment blocks and shopping malls have replaced old lanes where extended families lived. New roads have reshaped the pattern of familiar streets. In this way, Shanghai resembles most cities in Asia: the altered decor suggests to the people that they have indeed migrated, even if they have remained where they were born. The demolition of a known environment, and its reconstruction in an image of city from elsewhere, is bound to disturb those disoriented by the pace of changes they never sought. The old acknowledge the spectacular economic gains – these are inscribed in the changing topography of their living spaces; but as in other countries, they are left to absorb the social, psychological and spiritual costs.

The official version of ageing in China is similar to that heard in the Western countries: the elderly are a precious resource of the society, policies in favour of the aged will benefit everyone, their contribution must be recognised and rewarded. In practice, the principal means of combating the negative effects of ageing lies in economic growth – perhaps the most convincing evidence that whatever China professes ideologically, the true object of its faith is no different from that of the West.

Zhang Benbo also gestures to those 'Asian values' of which some leaders – notably Mahathir Mohamad in Malaysia – continue to boast.

> With abundant human resources and comparatively small social burdens, the first decade of the twenty-first century is a golden time for the country to get ready for the peak of the ageing population. In tapping human resources, training opportunities should also be provided for the old and middle-aged. Under China's special circumstances, care in the family home should remain the basic mode of care for the elderly. Such a tradition has been preserved throughout East Asia. Under the huge pressure of an ageing population, even industrialized countries have realized the flaws of solely relying on the social security system for elderly care, and have begun to encourage more families to take part. However, social services will gradually take responsibility for many functions still

> carried out in the family home. In big cities, the combination of care in the family home and community-based service will help the urban-based to live with ease and enjoy the love and care of both their family and community.[1]

The rhetoric of almost every country in the world converges: lengthening years of work, private provision for old age, the resilience of families, together with vague postures towards enhancing respect for the elderly, 'policies' to promote active ageing, which will provide older people with self-esteem and a sense of purpose. Who can disagree with all that?

Declaratory, aspirational and hortatory utterances from the United Nations, international agencies, governments, non-governmental organisations and charities are all very well. They set a tone, create a climate, change the atmosphere in which such matters are discussed. But they do *not* produce any measurable effect upon the dynamic of a global economy which makes its way in the world according to other rules than the needs of the elderly, the children, the disabled, the poor, or any of the other 'losers' in the great gamble of globalism. Everyone who works with the elderly knows that the energies, the accumulated knowledge, skills and competence of people over 55 constitute a vital resource for the world. Yet there is no mechanism to release or to deploy those powers for the benefit of humanity. The elderly are like a rich vein of ore that lies untapped in the field of a landowner who would rather let it remain in the ground to enhance the value of his property than open it up for the good of all.

In China, as elsewhere, people turn away from these intractable issues and do what they can to improve life for themselves and their neighbours in the localities where daily life, after all, must be lived. On January 22, 2001, ABC News reported on an initiative in Shanghai, where an elderly care programme called 'Time Bank' has been introduced. It is a little like a savings account, where vigorous, younger pensioners volunteer their time to take care of elderly people in need. The hours worked are registered in the neighbourhood. When the caregiver grows older, he or she will be entitled to the same hours of care from another volunteer. 'She is 92 and growing frail, but Cha Yueqiao still lives by herself. She lives without fear because every day, like clockwork, her neighbour and caregiver, Wu Peipei – who is 52 – will arrive to keep her company, help her with chores and take her shopping.' This effort seeks to provide care as close as possible to that traditionally given by the family. It also uses the energies of the young elderly. There is presently a construction boom in retirement homes in China. In the Beijing area alone, more than 300 were being built in January 2001.

A second example comes from a new service in the city of Dalian in the north-east of China. Retired teachers and students are being hired to visit the elderly for an hourly fee, which is paid by the children of the older person who may have had to move to distant parts of the country for employment, or whose hours of work may make it impossible to give adequate care to their parents. Although on a small scale, it is easily replicable. Zhang Yuteng, who founded the service, believes that everyone benefits, including the children of those visited, since it relieves them of anxiety over the well-being of their parents. The maximum number of visits by one individual to each elderly 'customer' is two 'to avoid any complicated attachments being formed'.[2]

Such initiatives are found in virtually every country in the world, from Adopt-A-Granny schemes to good neighbour clubs, from associations of caregivers and neighbourhood charities. They represent self-conscious efforts to recreate patterns of care which were part of organic networks of belonging. In the wider context, these may be seen as exercises in nostalgia, attempts to restore the irrecoverable, but they do at least two very positive things. First, they help the immediate beneficiaries, providing comfort where otherwise none would exist. Secondly, they show up the destructive power of the market, in places where it has broken local webs of belonging, without supplying people with the wealth to buy in alternatives the market can provide.

LAOS

A report by the Department of Labour and Social Welfare in Laos, conducted with the support of HelpAge International and CUSO, a Canadian development non-governmental organisation, recently investigated the position of the elderly in some poor rural parts of Laos. Laos stands at number 136 out of 176 on the United Nations Development Index.

Its findings confirm a worldwide trend, namely, that the contribution of the elderly, both to family well-being and to social survival, is considerable, but largely unrecognised, *even by themselves*. Women in particular, labour until the very end of their lives, which in Laos is two and a half years longer for women than men. Life expectancy in Laos in 1998 was 51.7 years. (This masks great regional differences – in Vientiane, the capital, it was 62.6, but in Sekong, the poorest province, only 35.)

If many older people underestimate their own abilities, this is partly *because they can no longer do as much as they once could*. They measure themselves against their own youth and are bound to see a falling away of their strength. This natural sense of loss is aggravated by the higher educational status of the young: this devalues their experience, and they come increasingly to see themselves as superfluous, a burden to the families to whose support they are essential. Even the very old stay and guard the house, look after the children and keep them from harm, perform domestic duties; yet they see their very presence as an inconvenience. The young do not share this perception. They know that mature people, the young elderly women, are among the most hard-working in the community, just as their male equivalents have experience in resolving disputes and family quarrels. Older men have a public voice, which women rarely possess.

In extremely poor societies, the pressures of survival weigh upon everyone. In rural Laos, there is usually a shortage of rice for several months (three to seven, depending on the locality and the fertility of the earth). Wells frequently run dry in the hot season, and diseases in poultry and animals occur each year. Although the people of the villages do not allow anyone to go homeless or remain uncared for when sick, older women often spend much time in the forest looking for food (almost half of Laos is still covered with forest). Older women are often the last repositories of knowledge of strategies for hungry seasons; their knowledge is precious to communities living close to the margin of existence.

In Laos, a direct correlation was found between the remoteness of the village and respect for the elderly. Where social change was slow, people showed a higher regard for their seniors; but where communications had improved, and there was ready access to the markets in Vientiane, many older people had experienced a decline in the respect accorded them. The most urgent desires of the elderly themselves were very modest – adequate food, water and a source of income; while their aspirations were equally undemanding – proper health care, and small funding for some economic activity, poultry-raising or fishponds. Older people remain a source of traditional health-care practices, including herbal medicines, birthing and spiritual healing, although this is everywhere being displaced by a preference for allopathic medicines.

The needs expressed in the study also reflect the needs of the whole community: it is not that the needs of the elderly are any different from those of others – they are simply more acutely felt. The issues are remarkably consistent across cultures, inflected only by accidents of geography and levels of development.

VIETNAM

In a participatory research programme conducted by HelpAge International in Vietnam, older people said 'respect for older people, especially the poor, was rapidly diminishing. Even for those older people who are cared for by their children, *respect may not accompany care*. Older people said that their children did look after them, but do not know, and never ask, what they are thinking... Since they perceive themselves as dependent upon their children, they ask them for as little as possible. Older people, especially older women, said they do not have any choice but to accept their changed position and status... If the older person remains "capable", in other words, able to continue to do farm work, heavy work and earn income, then their decision-making role is not diminished. Likewise, older people with material goods and assets were seen to keep their role as "head of household".'[3]

Another significant element in the report is that, once more, the importance of older women to maintenance of the household is not acknowledged. Indeed, as they age, the work of women declines less sharply than that of men, since many continue to work in the fields, collect animal dung for sale, gather fallen paddy at harvest time, burn charcoal, weed crops, pick up firewood for sale, grow vegetables, raise pigs, work as domestics – all activities for which they will earn something. Later, when this is beyond them, they will still work in the family home, preparing food, minding the children, washing clothes, boiling water, collecting fodder for pigs or buffaloes, cleaning, sewing and mending. As more young people migrate seasonally, the work of elders increases, and they may be required to take full responsibility for the home and children. This often coincides with a failing of their own strength, which only increases the pressure upon them.

In spite of this, the word 'burden' is perhaps the most frequently heard word in any language when the elderly refer to themselves. Perhaps it is because their work receives so little recognition that the elderly often feel *guilt*. They say they have lived too long. They feel they have no right to remain when so many of their contemporaries have gone. In the song by Jacques Brel, 'Les Vieux', he says the old must always apologise for not having moved on faster than they can. Elderly people regularly say, 'We are living on borrowed time.' Coupled with this self-effacement is also a high degree of stoicism, since even in the West, today's elderly were born to the rigid discipline and unrelenting rhythms of industrialism.

In Vietnam, where 20 years of war from 1954 to 1975, with its loss of 3 million people and untold privation and suffering, weakened everyone, health was undermined by war injuries from bombs and gas attacks as well as hunger and fear. It also led the people to expect very little of life, so that even an impoverished peace was a relief from the decades of violence and loss. Some say they wonder whether such a capacity for endurance will characterise younger generations.

The Vietnam report makes a distinction which is visible worldwide – between old age in the country and old age in the city. In the countryside, where almost 80 per cent of Vietnamese still live, the most significant problem articulated by the elderly poor was shortage of food, whereas in the slums of Ho Chi Minh, money was the first priority. As surpluses go from the countryside to feed increasing concentrations of urban dwellers, the very subsistence of the rural poor is impaired – by loss of land, by debt, by decreasing soil fertility, by medical expenses. Migration to the local big town or major cities is a response to the degradation of rural life, where money becomes the principal source of survival rather than food grown in the locality. This has a profound effect upon the sensibility of older people; upon those who stay back in the village to look after the children, and upon those who go with the family to a precarious dwelling in Hanoi or Ho Chi Minh.

An elderly farmer in Malaysia once said to me, 'People who grow their own food on their own land, without having to buy in the market, are the only free people in the world. This is why we are under such pressure to sell our land. They want us to give up our independence, because this stops the progress of the market.' This man was forced to sell his land because it was on the site of a proposed golf course. He said, 'The last harvest yielded by land is a pocketful of dollars. After that, it becomes barren.'

SOUTH AFRICA

The apartheid era made it impossible for the vast majority of people to prepare for their old age. They are the survivors of a social and economic disaster; and to compound the problems, the transition from the apartheid system to a market economy has limited the areas of action open to government. While it has sought to eliminate some of the distortions of the apartheid years, it is doing so in a global environment that is unfavourable to redistribution. This, together with the AIDS disaster, has imposed new constraints on those who might, perhaps, have expected more immediate and more tangible relief from the multiple injustices of racial, economic and social exclusion.

Older people, especially women, play a prolonged caring, even parenting, role in the family well into old age. Many continue to work and make an important contribution to the family income. Their pension, too, is also usually pooled in the collective resources of the family, especially when there are so many young unemployed. In research conducted for HelpAge International by Thebe Mohatle and Robert de Graft Agyarko in July 1999, it emerged that some households depend solely upon the pensions of the elderly. Pensions, means-tested and non-contributory, of a maximum of R.260, have a high take-up rate and constitute two-thirds of social transfers in the South African budget. Even so, black people receive a disproportionately lower share of the total than would be fair (although making up about 75 per cent of the population, they receive just over 50 per cent of the money allocated to pensions).

This is explained, in part, by the fact that, although the pension is crucial to tens of thousands of families, many fail to draw it. The bureaucratic path to gaining access (up to seven documents are needed), poor administration, the length of time required to process applications, the distance individuals must travel to collect it, everything conspires to complicate the distribution of what people are entitled to.

The research found that the major part of the pension is spent on food and school fees. Although older people traditionally look to the family as the main source of support and care, they are now finding themselves stretched to the limit by responsibilities which no one else is capable of assuming. Their role has become crucial. Old age homes do exist, but they are perceived as the last resort, only for the neglected and abandoned. As in other parts of Africa, the toll of AIDS has made the elderly into carers of last resort; a role which they, with all the oppression and privation they have seen, is, surely, almost too hard to bear.

The social and economic wounds of apartheid have left scars which are not going to be healed by even the most benign form of market economics. In 1995, the economically active population was estimated at around 14.4 million (out of 42 million people: this means every working person must take care of herself and two others). The South African Institute of Race Relations estimated in 1997 that at least 22 per cent of the economically active were employed in the informal sector. The unemployment rate was 24 per cent (41 per cent for blacks, 23 per cent for Asians, 17 per cent for coloureds, and 5 per cent for whites). In the formal sector, blacks earn 13 per cent of the income earned by whites – one of the most distorted income distribution profiles in the world. Twenty-three per cent of black households were in the lowest income category (1 per cent of whites), while 65 per cent of whites, but only 10 per cent of blacks, were in the highest category.

Although health care is available at primary health-care centres, these are often badly equipped and have few facilities for anything more than the most basic treatment. Free medicine is not available for the characteristic chronic conditions and ailments of older people. There is little specialised medical care for the elderly, who are given a lower priority than mothers and children.

Throughout the country in the communities where the research was conducted, there are different linguistic terms to designate the various categories of old. In the poor Northern Province, there are words meaning 'old but still able to care for him/herself'; and a separate category suggesting one who is frail, vulnerable and dependent. In Kwa Zulu, there is young old; old old and very old. In Katlehong near Johannesburg, words indicating grandmother/father and old woman/man are distinct from those meaning great-grandmother/father and great-great grandmother/father, all suggesting various degrees of progressive weakness.

The report states that there is ambiguity in attitudes towards the elderly. Their role in holding the family together through all the vicissitudes of apartheid coexists with increasing abuse of the elderly – physical, emotional and financial.

Some of these conflicts arise out of the past, but others are a result of a country emerging from the monstrosity of apartheid into a system the primary aim of which is not social justice. This must be subordinated to the creation of wealth. The neo-liberal model of globalisation embodies the view that the relief of poverty may be achieved only through the generation of wealth and not through the redistribution of the wealth that already exists. This is not what the struggle against apartheid envisaged in its years of exile, imprisonment and brutalisation. The high level of crime in post-apartheid South Africa reflects the distortion of priorities that have come with freedom. The same is true of Russia and other former Communist states. The world into which oppressed peoples have entered disadvantages the weak and the poor; among whom, everywhere, the elderly are prominent.

THE CASE OF GERMANY

Germany, despite having more than 4 million unemployed in 2002, faces the option of immigration or immiseration.

On present trends, the falling birth rate of Germany will lead to more than half its people being over 60 by 2050. The population of the country will fall by between 16 and 23 million from its present level of 82 million.

In response to this grim outlook for the world's third most prosperous country, in July 2001 the independent Sussmuth

Commission recommended radical changes in immigration policy. Until now, Germany has maintained the fiction that its foreign workers are *Gastarbeiter*, guest workers, even though many of these – 27 per cent are from Turkey – have now established families in the country. There are 7.3 million people of non-German origin in Germany, including about 2 million born there. This represents more than 9 per cent of the population and is the highest proportion in Europe.

In spite of persistently high unemployment, the Sussmuth Commission report suggests that Germany should allow 50,000 workers from outside the European Union to enter the country. Some would be permitted to settle, and the denial that Germany is a place of permanent settlement would be abandoned. Among the newcomers, 20,000 would qualify for permanent residence; temporary visas would be offered to a further 20,000, with 10,000 for foreign trainees. There would be easier procedures for top business people, scientists and artists earning 90,000 euros or more per year. There would also be 'improved social integration', including 600 hours of German lessons for each migrant.

Increased immigration will not reverse the trend of a falling and ageing population, but will slow it down. The information technology industry is short of 75,000 workers, while the hotel and catering sector requires 80,000 semi-skilled people.

The German government introduced a law in March 2002 giving effect to these recommendations, but it was thrown out by the Constitutional Court in December 2002.

Chapter 5

ACTIVE AGEING

The common wisdom is now contained in the concept of 'active ageing.' This itself contains some interesting ambiguities. Does it mean a kind of therapeutic occupation for the elderly, or a positive participation in the work of society? Does it involve a restoration of the effaced function of the elderly? Does it mean that the elderly are now the new 'reserve army of labour'?

At the present time, in the West the elderly are an object of considerable interest to advertisers and marketing agencies, since many enjoy a reasonable disposable income. This places the elderly essentially in the category of consumers. This is not the same thing as releasing the energy and powers that remain unproductive and on which no claims are made.

A generation has come to retirement in the last quarter of the twentieth century in the expectation of generous pension provision and access to much improved health care. To some extent, the spectacular increase in material well-being in the West has compensated older people for a certain loss of power and moral authority. It is easier to adapt to convulsive technological and social change, as well as to shifts in values, if people enjoy a certain measure of comfort and financial security. Indeed, this may conceal significant forfeits and losses, which may go virtually unnoticed among the very tangible gains.

A recent policy brief from the Organisation for Economic Co-Operation and Development[1] offers some clues to official thinking in the rich Western societies. The paper recognises that the retired in nine OECD countries receive an average of about 80 per cent of the income of those still in work, a relatively small reduction in the standard of living. This is a consequence of occupational pensions and a core state pension which, with means-tested benefits, mitigates the poverty of the poorest old. It then goes on to discuss the 're-balancing of time spent in and out of work'. This is a euphemism for raising the retirement age. The other necessary 'reform' is also described as 're-balancing' of the provision of pension, away from state-funded and occupation-based to 'personal' pensions. Once more, it involves a weakening of security: that feasibility of such a development depends upon continuing economic growth and a high yield on investments (in other words an act of faith) is casually mentioned in a couple of throwaway lines. Stripped of euphemisms, it means that the future elderly will make their own private settlement with global capital; in other words, a return to the good old days when it was a concern neither of the state nor of employers to protect workers against the time when they could no longer labour.

Such truths are not spelt out because they are politically unacceptable. After all, the prosperity of the past half century has also changed the psyche and the sensibility of the elderly. Frugality, thought for the future, saving, setting something aside for the rainy day – such values are quite at odds with the squandering and spendthrift lifestyle, in which 'consumer confidence' is the highest moral imperative. Difficult discussions are elided in what are presented as matters of mere policy, when they suggest a reversal of everything that has occurred over the last two generations.

HOW HAVE THE ELDERLY CHANGED?

Perhaps the surest sign that they have indeed understood the ebbing of their authority is to be seen in the way the elderly come more and more to mimic the young. The leisured elderly are major contributors to the growth of what is now the biggest global industry, namely, tourism and travel. Accompanying the discovery of experiences undreamed-of in their earlier life, there is a growing pursuit of the prolongation of youth.

This, too, is not a new idea. It has haunted the earliest myths of humanity, from the apples of youth with which the goddess Iduna kept the gods perpetually young in the Asgard of Norse mythology, to the contemporary advertising industry, which offers 'anti-ageing' creams, potions, oils and medicaments, some of them taken from exotic plants and shrubs known to the ancient world. What is new is the turning of the quest for eternal youth into a profitable industrial concern. The elderly are major clients of the beauty and cosmetics industries. They are important consumers of elective surgery, interventions to halt or reverse the ageing process. Certain iconic figures demonstrate the possibility, not merely of graceful, but even of *sexy*, ageing: Joan Collins, the late Barbara Cartland, Marlene Dietrich, Zsa Zsa Gabor have offered to the world an acting out of the familiar subjective feeling of being unchanged despite the effects of time. It is noteworthy that this has been essentially a model for women to aspire to, although recently men, too, have been caught up in similar projects to deny the effects of age.

PENSIONERS AND THE RETIRED

The way the elderly see themselves is still at odds with wider social perceptions. This, too, complicates efforts to reabsorb them into gainful occupations. The old are regarded in industrial society as *pensioners*. This is itself a reductive and diminishing designation: a pensioner remains a dependant, paid what is due to her or him on relinquishing duties fulfilled, or in recognition of past labour. The word also has valedictory connotations, which suggests they are waiting for the end. This itself is part of a generally patronising or facetious tone that governs a majority of references to older people – the euphemisms of 'senior citizens' or 'elders' still bear faint traces of a fallen patriarchy, those who have borne the heat and burthen of the day. Old folk dwell (the middle class reside, the young live). Retirees have withdrawn from life. They have fulfilled their 'superannuation' schemes and sit comfortably awaiting the term of their actuarially calculated life. The aged are banished even further from the circle of the living. They wander aimlessly through the labyrinths of nostalgia or down winding memory lanes, recalling the olden days: old fogeys, old maids, old boys, old stagers. They tell old stories in an old-fashioned way. They are behind the times, out of date. They have had their day.

It is in reaction against these negative stereotypes that self-help organisations of older people have come into existence – in Britain there are over 1 million pensioners in local groups or trade union associations. The University of the Third Age has thousands of students. Saga is a commercial enterprise providing services to the elderly at reduced prices. Concessions are granted for cheaper travel, in places of entertainment and at public events. The government has introduced a winter fuel allowance for all over 60. Income supplements are available to the poorest, even though there are still some proud elderly people who regard their entitlements as 'charity' and refuse to claim them. Age Concern and Help the Aged are charities dedicated to advocacy and campaigning on behalf of the elderly, while HelpAge International works globally on issues of ageing all over the world. 1999 was declared by the United Nations to be the Year of the Older Person, and October 1 is designated as the Day of the Older Person. In the declaration of 1999, Towards a Society for All the Ages, Kofi Annan described the ageing of the world's population as 'humanity's coming of age'.

It shouldn't be difficult to recognise the contribution of the elderly to society, to acknowledge that their fate is that of all of us, if we live long enough. Yet almost everything officially uttered about the elderly is full of hollow moral imperatives and prescriptions. The harder reality outlined by the OECD remains buried beneath pieties: indeed, the elderly probably generate more pious exhortation than any other group apart from children.

For example, the 2002 HelpAge International report, *The State of the World's Older People*,[2] lists ten actions to end age discrimination. These are completely unexceptionable. No humane person would dissent from any of them; but there is no indication of the agency whereby this is going to be accomplished. Here they are.

1. Recognise the human rights of older people and the benefits of population ageing for human development.
2. Allocate older people their fair share of national and global resources.
3. Guarantee adequate social protection and minimum income in old age.
4. Provide accessible and free health care for older people
5. Make credit, employment, training and education schemes available to people regardless of age.
6. Put an end to violence against older people.
7. Ensure policy-makers listen to and act on the views of older people.

8. Include and consult older people in emergency aid and rehabilitation planning after disasters and humanitarian crises.
9. Establish international practice standards to govern policy on ageing.
10. Support older people in their role as carers.

Who is going to put all this into effect? For these aspirations strike at a world system in which a 'fair share' of national or global resources is far from its central purpose. Who is going to allocate these resources? Certainly not the market, which has sensors that respond only to where the money is, not to where need is located. Who is going to put an end to violence to old people? The neglect and disuse of the skills and powers of the elderly is itself a form of violence, and this is built into the very structures of injustice to which 'we' must look for redress.

The fate of the United Nations' first call for children in 1990 has remained largely in the realm of theory. Why should resolutions for the aged fare better?

Perhaps local initiatives are more successful. After all, these focus, not on moral generalities, but on the places where lives are lived.

In 1998, Age Concern England (the National Council on Ageing) published a response to the British Government's Strategy for Neighbourhood Renewal (1997), which appeared to have excluded the elderly from any active role in the strategy. Age Concern states, 'In 1996, 18.1 per cent of the population of the UK (10,668,000 people) were over pensionable age. People often refer to the "elderly" as if they were a single group of people, but their needs are as varied as those of any other group in the population.' Older people constitute 38 per cent of council tenants and 18.7 per cent of single older people over 60 lived in sub-standard housing. Older people's incomes are among the lowest. Although between 1979 and 1997 the average net income of pensioners rose by 64 per cent, this masked considerable variations (the richest fifth saw an increase of 85 per cent and the poorest fifth only 22 per cent). Crime and the fear of crime feature at the top of the list of older people's worries, even though the chance of becoming a victim of crime over the age of 60 decreases sharply. The level of crime, however, in deprived neighbourhoods is well above the national average, and the fear of crime in these areas seriously affects the well-being of older people.

The Age Concern report advocates, among other things, using 'the knowledge, skills and experience of older people as a resource for developing and running local learning programmes'. These should combine training in modern vocational skills and new technology for older people who are unemployed and who wish to work. The learning needs of older people belonging to black and ethnic minority communities should be clearly identified and addressed with appropriate programmes. People over the age of 50 now account for 30 per cent of consumer spending. Appropriate services to ensure the retention of their money in the community they live in should be provided. Older people should be consulted and involved in the work of local Crime and Disorder partnerships and these should include specific measures aimed at developing crime prevention strategies that will reduce crime and the fear of crime among older people. Local strategic partnerships should monitor the gaps in provision of leisure services to older people. They should ensure that leisure facilities are designed to meet the demographic cultural, physical and spiritual diversity of the community and promote healthier living, cross-cultural and intergenerational activities. Improvements in mechanisms to enable older people to access housing, health, education and leisure facilities are recommended, with adequate transport to 'reduce isolation'.

There is much more; all of it highly desirable, calculated to confer dignity upon the elderly. But it seems that, even at the local level, much of the rhetoric is about what should be done, what ought to happen, what 'we' must do. The problem with both abstract resolutions and practical commitment to such strategies, plans and schemes, with their upbeat, can-do assumptions is that, at every turn, they hit against the harsher cultural realities of a market-driven society.

We live in a world which increasingly admires youth, glamour, fashion, success, money, power and fame. The iconic status of celebrities hovers over everything, a luminous and ubiquitous presence which eclipses and disgraces age, experience, wisdom and kindness alike. The sexualisation of society, by definition, excludes older people. This undermines the exhortation and optimism of official agencies and their gesturings to concern, humanity and inclusion. We have all been placed under the sign of the market which, although it appears in no zodiac, is now the major determinant on all our destinies. It erodes respect for age, it subverts the traditional and the customary, it mocks failure, weakness and decrepitude. It doesn't want to hear bad news. It will not tolerate debility or neediness. The best efforts – and they are sometimes heroic – of government initiatives and voluntary agencies alike are often weakened or nullified by an obsession with youth, beauty and fame. The forces working against the elevation of the elderly are very powerful, and result in a kind of paralysis, which is why everyone falls back upon rhetoric and posturing, or at best charitable local endeavours that create, not models for action, but discrete defensive islands of resistance in the prevailing culture.

The market is a more powerful influence in the lives of the elderly – as it is on everyone else – than any other. This development has accelerated within the last generation or so, and it reinforces the sense of the elderly that they have been marginalised; the removal of existing forms of state or employer protection in favour of the vagaries of the market is unlikely to create a greater feeling of security.

It seems that the status of the elderly will be raised only when it becomes clear to everyone that they are indispensable to economic survival. Plans to outlaw age discrimination and to raise the retirement age are disingenuously presented as liberation. With the declining value of pensions, the rhetoric about equality and dignity, the defence of the rights of the older person conceal a more coercive intention. This may, however, prove more effective than an official humanitarianism, which has so far failed to elevate the elderly in a society that belongs to the young and thrusting, the creators of wealth, makers of fortunes, the winners of globalisation.

ELDER ABUSE

Elder abuse is a relatively recent concern, both in the United States and Europe. In 1996 in the USA, it was estimated that a total of 551,011 persons aged 60 and over experienced abuse, neglect and/or self-neglect in domestic settings. Of the substantiated cases, Adult Protective Services assess that 49 per cent were cases of neglect, 35 per cent were emotional or psychological abuse, 30 per cent financial or material exploitation, 25 per cent physical abuse, 3.6 per cent abandonment, and 0.3 per cent sexual abuse. It is perhaps significant that there was a correlation between abuse and income – in general, poorer people suffered more neglect, psychological and physical abuse than higher income groups, although some of this may be due to more effective concealment by the better off.

In a sensitive analysis of the causes of elder abuse, Linda M. Woolf[3] of Webster University lists caregiver stress, the condition of dependency or impairment of the older person, external stress, social isolation, intergenerational transmission of violence and intra-individual dynamics or personal problems of the abuser. Caring for an adult who is sick, confused or infirm is an extremely demanding job. Loved ones can easily be goaded beyond endurance by what sometimes appears perverseness, while those employed to look after strangers may have little training or competence in responding to their needs. As dependency increases, so do the resentment and exasperation of caregivers. Abuse is more common against people in ill health than against the healthy, and against those elders on whom the carer is financially dependent. Abuse is more common in families who are socially isolated. Children who were abused are also more likely to abuse their own parents when they become the principal caregiver. Caregivers who suffer from alcoholism, drug addiction or emotional disorders are also more likely to become abusers.

Although crimes against the elderly remain low as a proportion of crime, a few publicised cases reinforce the fears of older people. In this fear we can perhaps also detect recognition by the elderly of the declining respect in which they are held.

The old demonstrate to us our own fate. The presence of so many elderly in the streets, the shopping malls, in buses and public spaces offer an inescapable spectacle of what we will become. The young, the healthy, the vigorous for the most part exist side by side with the old, ignoring them, looking through them, sometimes jostling them, sometimes making way for them or offering assistance in crossing the road or surrendering a seat in the train. It is in many ways understandable that this constant image of our best hopes for the future (the worst being that we might not get there at all) sometimes moves us to irritation or anger. It is not that there has been any great increase in crimes against the elderly, but older people are disparaged, overlooked, disregarded, isolated. How can the young – who after all are the supreme arbiters of values in the global market – be expected to show solicitude for those who stand in their way in their feverish and urgent desire to reach a future that holds the fulfilment of all their desires, particularly when that future also contains a foreshadowing of things to come, in the frail and elderly all around them?

Of course, the opposite is also true: we may equally discern in the infirmity and dependency of older people the ghost of our own loved parents and grandparents. It is perhaps simply that the stories of compassion and dedication to the old do not reach the pages of newspapers or the TV news as outrages against the elderly do. In many parts of the world, older people are regularly addressed by strangers in the inclusive terms of kinship – grandmother, grandfather, mother, father, aunt and uncle. Whatever weakening of authority and power may have occurred, the reservoir of affection and goodwill to those who have nurtured us remains.

CRIME AND THE ELDERLY

The United States Department of Justice findings on Crimes Against Older Persons 1992–1997[4] should allay the fear of crime among the elderly. There were only five crimes per 1,000 people over 65, against more than 100 for the under-25s. Nine out of ten crimes against the elderly were property crimes – 117 for every 1,000 people, against 480 per 1,000 of younger people. The only area of crime where the elderly were as likely to be victims as the rest of the population was in purse-snatching or pick-pocketing.

In 1997, 12.7 per cent of the people of the US were over 65; 1.4 million of them were in a home or a long-term care facility. The number of murders of those over 65 decreased between 1992 and 1997 from 0.56 per 10,000 to 0.27 per 10,000. There were three murders of over-65s in every 100,000 people. When it comes to assault, the least likely victims were elderly females (4 per 1,000), and the most likely young white males (126 per 1,000).

This does not, however, provide much comfort for the elderly who continue to express a high level of anxiety over violence. What they want, above all, is security.

The issue of security for older people has been a major recent issue in elections in Western Europe. This does not focus primarily upon an assurance of financial security, the certainty that the basic needs of the elderly will be met. Often stranded in older parts of the cities, in social housing, many are afraid to go out after dark, some even fearful of going out at all. This feeling of personal insecurity is fed by the media. Regular reports on TV and in local newspapers tell of an old-age pensioner being mugged on her way home from the chip shop for the sake of a few pounds in her purse; an old man has a heart attack when he surprises an intruder in his home; a woman of 80 is raped in her own bedroom. A picture appears on screen of a woman's face, eyes blackened, violet and yellow contusions on her face, the consequence of trying to resist a thief only a few metres from her own home.

A pervasive *iconography of insecurity* is diffused into every home; it increases fear especially among those who live alone. Demands are constant for stricter policing, tougher sentencing for criminals, not only by the elderly, but by their children and relatives who are no longer in a position to look after them. It is true that most people remain emotionally close to their elderly parents. 'I only have to pick up the phone and they'll come straight away' is a frequent comment. But it has become axiomatic for many people that, although they love them dearly, they cannot bear to live with them. A form of disengagement that is not indifference increasingly governs our relationships with parents. 'We invite her for Sunday dinner, I pop in two or three times a week, but she's better off in her own home, she wants her independence, she's too set in her ways, she wouldn't be happy, she prefers it this way.' And many elderly reiterate the alibis from another perspective – 'they're too busy, they've got their own lives to lead, they can't be worrying about me all the time, I've got everything I want here, this is my home'; and the crimson cyclamen wilts in its pot in the heat of the gas fire, and the pictures of the grandchildren, bright and smiling against a cerulean background of a school photograph surround them in the pool of light spread by the reading lamp behind the winged armchair, in which they spend more and more time sleeping, as the tea grows cold in its cup and the daily paper falls, crumpled, to the floor...

The fracturing of the *physical* – if not emotional – cohesion of the family, the great increase in the numbers of elderly people living alone, the survival of so many widows, deflect the meaning of 'security' from concerns with shelter, food, health care, warmth, comfort and social participation of the elderly to 'security', meaning safety from attack. In this way, security comes to mean more money spent on policing, investment in locks, bolts, grills and chains in people's homes rather than on that which comes from the presence of loved flesh and blood. Just as, nationally, 'security' now suggests the build-up of weaponry and armaments, so for the individual it indicates the defensive construction of a safe haven against the menace, real or imaginary, of the ill will, rapacity and cruelty of the predators, addicts and muggers who prowl the streets outside.

A WORLD GROWING OLD

I used the phrase 'a world growing old' to suggest something more than a question of demography. It hints, too, at the exhaustion of the planet, a world abused, mistreated and exploited. The very processes that have lengthened life expectancy have also contributed to a using up of the resources of earth – the fossil fuels, the fertility of the soil, the purity of the waters. The long-term effects of the 30,000 or so chemicals in daily use are far from known; carcinogens may already have damaged the gene pool of humanity; while global warming itself threatens the fabric of the planet. It is possible that the regenerative capacity of the world itself has been impaired by the achievement of a 'standard of living', which is the greatest achievement of more than two centuries of an intensive industrialism. Here is another epic paradox: more and more people live on, even while the life-support system – the biosphere – which sustains all social and economic systems may itself be fundamentally impaired.

Technology promises to lengthen life even further. Genetic manipulation, the growing ability to screen out inherited characteristics that condemn people to sicknesses that shorten life, the possibility of reservoirs of individual stem-cell tissue – all this presages even more years on earth: a kind of provisional immortality. At the same time, the economic system which produces these wonders and miracles weighs with ever greater force and pressure on the resource-base which nourishes them.

The speeding up of the application of new technologies has epochal implications for the moral and social wealth stored up in old age, where knowledge born of poverty and scarcity had accumulated over time. The reservoir of knowing what to do in the face of shortage, insufficiency and hardship – the vast unreckoned creativity of the poor – has been disgraced by the new knowledge. The young have grown to another world, other expectations – to promises of wealth and hope engendered by industrialism and its formidable productive power. One important effect of this has been that older knowledge systems have been superseded. The old have been transformed from the possessors of strategies vital for survival into relics of the past, whose wisdom and experience will never again be needed. In many societies, this has brought about an abrupt reversal of roles, so that the young become the instructors of their elders, the interpreters of the new culture into which all have migrated, whether or not they have moved from the places where they were born.

This is even more dramatic in the case of those who have indeed migrated to another country, a different culture. Europe and North America now contain millions of people who, only yesterday, were peasants. Their awe and incomprehension of the altered environment, and their inability to master the language of their new home, places them at the mercy of their children who, mobile and inventive, lead them by the hand through the city traffic, mediate on their behalf with bureaucracy and officialdom, translate the documents that come through the letterbox, guide them through the traps and pitfalls of the outside world.

This is also the case with those who have migrated internally from the small towns and villages into the cities of the South. Old people look wonderingly at the primary colours of McDonald's in Jakarta and Bangkok, unsure how to open the polystyrene container in which the hamburger nestles; and they marvel at the dexterity of the fingers of their grandchildren as they play with the electronic game, and they look down at their own hands in shame, fingers clumsy and blunted from having used the tools that dig the earth, sowed seeds and scratched the weeds that invade the crops. The grandchildren know that their lives are never going to be like that, and they pity their elders, and are sometimes consumed by a loving shame at their vulnerability.

AGEING CULTURES

Cultures, too, have grown old and are dying everywhere. Languages are becoming extinct, folk wisdom and ancient proverbs freeze on the lips of the last representatives of traditional cultures; and the memories of herbal medicines, starvation foods, of triumph over adversity and survival, remain unspoken, consigned like the archaic and picturesque rituals surrounding birth, sickness and death to the notebooks of ethnographers or confided, for the last time, to the tape-recorders of makers of documentaries on a vanished world.

Ancient self-reliant cultures all over the world have faltered under the influence of industrial culture, first through colonialism, later through its socialist variant, and more recently, through the assault of globalisation. The Adivasis (tribals) were the original inhabitants of India. Their millennial cultures had sustained themselves in the same places until disturbed by a system which demanded that they transform into money all the free gifts of the forest which provided everything they needed. The imposition of the cash economy on ancient cultures was an act of destructive violence. The British – and later, the Forest Department of free India – destroyed the trees and extracted the resources which had been the object of ancient animist beliefs, some of them of great beauty and antiquity. The Adivasis had seen divine spirits in the features of the landscape that supported their well-being. Once these were destroyed, so too was faith in the nurturing environment. They were ready for 'conversion' – to Christianity, Hinduism, Islam.

They still remain with the wreckage of broken cultures, from which the young have departed for the cities, to work as labourers, rickshaw drivers and servants, and take to alcohol, drugs and sex as consolations for their grief and exile. Just as many old people die of loss, so the life expectancy of many indigenous peoples has been shortened by loss of meaning and faith – this was the fate of the North American indigenous people and the Aboriginals, and all the inheritors of cultures effaced, sometimes with great violence, by the modern world. Their knowledge systems have been wiped out, just as the wisdom and experience of the old worldwide has become an irrelevance in the presence of the superior *knowingness* of the culture of globalism.

In north Bangladesh and eastern India, where the Shantals were the first tribals to rise against the British, the old are haunted by the memories of a proud and self-reliant culture which, although destroyed before they were, nevertheless maintained some of ancient customs and practices. They started work at the age of seven or eight, minding cattle, a twig in their hand, watching with envy the work of eating which was the destiny of cows and buffaloes. Old men remember receiving food or clothing as wages. The half-demolished jungles are the ruins of their civilisation. They say, 'We worshipped the trees and the flowers and the animals. The foreigners came and cut down our trees, emptied the land of all that grew. Now they come back to us and say, "Why did you cut down your trees, you have ruined your environment. We shall give you a grant to replant the forests." But they know nothing of the richness and variety of what grew here. They plant timber, not trees.'

Silence is the natural element of the depleted countryside. The call of birds, the cries of insects, tiny sounds of barely detectable creatures. The footfalls of passing daily labourers crunch dry twigs sharp as bone; a whisper of straw stirs in the breeze. The faint rasp of leaves scrapes the brushed earth of a courtyard; the chewing of cattle, the vibration of a bird's wing, the creaking of a tree, the scratching of mice, the faint gargle of water in the throat of an ancient spring – these are the melancholy music of a dying culture.

The Garo language has retreated to domestic use, but Bengali is the language of instruction in the schools and of officialdom. In the villages, tranquil courtyards are shaded by fruit trees. The houses of clay are sculpted like an emanation of the grey earth itself. On the ground some newly boiled paddy has been laid on bamboo mats to dry. A woman walks through the grain, turning it over with her feet so that it will dry in the sun. Her ankles move gracefully, and pale dust and husks from the paddy blow in the wind. Grains cascade like beads over her smooth skin in the lemon sunlight.

Most of the people here are Christian, but their parents were animists. When they remember the old religion, the old people become alive in a different way. They evoke the other people they used to be, the different culture they inhabited, and which inhabited them: a metamorphosis of cultural being seems to take place before our eyes.

'They used to believe that if they sacrificed cattle, goats or hens, people would be cured of fever or other diseases. They made effigies out of paddy straw and sacrificed an animal to the gods of sickness. People appeased two gods, Shushun and Tattu, with drink and dancing.' They sing an old Garo song. 'It is a song for two voices, a man and a woman making love. The man sings, "To cut the paddy, we need a sickle, to get a young woman is no easy thing." The woman responds, "To play in harmony, you need a tune, to get a young woman is no easy thing." As they danced, they drank *chu*, which was filtered from fermented rice. At the time of a birth, the relatives would come and place a little *chu* in the baby's mouth. At a death, they would mourn together and burn the dead. Relatives made them new clothes for their journey into the next world. Now we bury our dead.'

The men, in particular, have been rendered functionless by the destruction of the forests. Animists, conservers and worshippers of trees and water and hills, they are evictees of a faith which was the life breath of the jungles. The men collected honey, wood and produce from the trees. It was their occupation, which was degraded by the felling of trees; they find comfort in the destructive compensation of alcohol. They drink *Bangla math*, a rice-based liquor. The women were the first to find solace in an alien religion: since they have responsibility for the next generation, they cannot transmit the despair of a worn and wasting culture, so they teach them about Jesus and his power to save them, although not from the decay of their blighted heritage, as they seek to salvage dignity and purpose from the ruins of an environment that has robbed them of millennial meaning.

Chapter 6

All over the world, many elderly and abandoned people find refuges in mosques, temples, gurudwaras and churches. Although charity cannot meet the vastness of need, hope and inspiration are sometimes to be found in the places where they are least expected. In May 2002, I visited a village called, appropriately, Gandhi Colony in Faridabad, which is a satellite city of Delhi.

> For the past 18 years, Balraj has nursed his sick wife. She is now almost completely paralysed. He has to lift her, feed and wash her. This is not an easy task. Since both have been leprosy patients, nothing but stumps remain of his hands. To raise her, he approaches the bed, and she clasps her arms around his neck, and the strength of his body raises her to an upright position.
>
> Balraj came from Chennai, where fear of leprosy still haunts village communities, and creates an untouchability of its own, no less stringent than that of caste. Even the family members of leprosy patients are sometimes forbidden to enter a village. Balraj sacrificed himself by leaving home, so that his relatives would not be contaminated by the stigma. He ceded his land to his brother, and resigned himself to a life of begging in Delhi, in North India, where the shame of leprosy is less corrosive. Even after all these years, there is no question of returning home.

If he now knows peace in Gandhi Colony, this is partly because of the support offered by an initiative taken 25 years ago by M. Gurappa and a group of fellow leprosy sufferers, who decided they would no longer live at the mercy of passers-by, harassed by police and the bureaucrats who sought to 'cleanse' the city during Mrs Gandhi's Emergency in the mid-1970s.

Faridabad is not a place you would ordinarily go to look for peace and security. A raw new settlement of perhaps one and a half million people. Rising in the rocky landscape around Delhi, it is the site of great skeletal structures of factory buildings and housing complexes, unmade roads and sudden blinding sandstorms.

Yet only a few metres from the main road, you find yourself in the middle of a village of single-storey, pink-painted houses with blue doors and windows and shaded by maturing neem trees. There is a dispensary, a community hall, a school, a temple, a handloom-weaving shed. There is a byre for about 30 cows, and a poultry farm which provides livelihood for some of the 220 recovered leprosy patients and their families who live here.

This is the Bharat Mata Kushth Ashram. It is not a place apart, but merges into the larger village of Gandhi Colony. Concrete middle-class flats shadow the almost rural thoroughfare, and the end of the ashram is marked only by a change in the colour of the buildings.

Most people are from Tamil Nad, Karnataka and Andhra Pradesh, a majority now elderly. They came north as voluntary exiles to spare families the presence of a shameful affliction. Many have lost contact with their relatives. Delhi offered them a place to beg; the ashram offers them a home.

Yamappa is almost 80, his sight drowned in the clear liquid of his eyes. Grey stubble on his cheeks, a check lunghi, he is one of the oldest people in the settlement. I met him in the community hall, where about 50 people had gathered. Some are frail and walk with a crutch or stick. Those who can work have achieved a sense of purpose – for many, this is the first job they have ever known, apart from begging. To have suffered from leprosy, to be elderly, but to be in possession of real work – this has raised pride and given dignity.

Gayamma, an alert woman of 72 in a peacock-blue blouse and pale saree, is from Andhra Pradesh. She came to Delhi 30 years ago with her husband who left his family to spare them the disgrace of leprosy. He begged until he became blind. Then she led him through the streets, begging on his behalf. They had no children. An older sister died recently in Rajasthan, where her only known relatives remain. She never sees them.

Not all the people in the village were affected by leprosy. Chembai has a large solemn face, grey hair and vague eyes, which hint at the profound melancholy of people driven both out f their home and their mind. Her husband's death sent her wandering, both physically and mentally, until someone directed her to the ashram. Those who cannot look after themselves are cared for by others. There is an instinctive pooling of the human resources, on which the most needy can rely, a sharing of the spirit, a kind of spontaneous socialism of instinct.

Since begging has been the principal occupation of most people, it is not easy to give it up, although it is now forbidden here. If anyone needs money, she or he must tell the group why it is required; if judged to be a necessary expenditure, it will be given.

Kanamma is a small thin woman, who walks with a stick: her right leg was withered by polio when she was a child. She used to wheel her husband in a rough handcart through the streets of Delhi. When he died, Kanamma worked as a maid, washing and cleaning floors in middle-class neighbourhoods. She now spins in the handloom factory, and earns enough money to buy her own food and prepare her own meals. For Kanamma, as for many others here, life was insecure, stranded between the mercy of strangers and the sidewalk of Delhi until she found the ashram.

G. Venugopal also works for the village. He is from Andhra Pradesh, and left home because his sister's marriage was cancelled when it became known that he had leprosy. 'Even now,' he says, 'there are notices in hotels in Andhra saying "Leprosy Patients Not Allowed". Even today many doctors will not treat us. If you are known to be the relative of a patient, you may also be banned from villages and public spaces. In North India there is less prejudice.'

M. Gurappa is president of the ashram, of which he was co-founder. He was born in Gulbarga in Karnataka; his father died when he was four, and his mother when he was twelve. Two older sisters married before their mother's death. A younger brother went to live with one of the sisters. Gurappa went to a Hindu boarding school, where fees were waived in view of his orphaned status. The school closed after a year and Gurappa served in the household of the *guru*, who was also an Ayurvedic doctor. At 17, he became aware that something was wrong. While making tea, he would scald himself but feel nothing. He went to an allopathic doctor for a check-up, and although the doctor never informed him of it, he knew from helping his Ayurvedic master that the medicine he was given was for leprosy.

He was advised to work in the fields. He returned to his sisters, who sent him to a leprosy hospital. There, he saw only handicapped people. Terrified, he would not even drink the water. He feared his hands and feet would also wear away. He ran from the place and worked as an agricultural day labourer. One day a thorn penetrated his foot, which became infected and swelled up. He left for Mumbai, but was refused admission to hospital. He lived on the streets for three days, fed by other leprosy sufferers on the station. He found work on a tea-stall, but after repeated burns to his hands, he left and began a life of begging.

His younger brother came to Mumbai to look for him. The brother got a job in the flower market for ten rupees a day (20 cents). He found a room where they could stay together. They ate one plate of rice between them each day. Gurappa decided to leave his brother: if he stayed with him, it would certainly spoil his life. 'I just left, without saying goodbye. I went back to begging on the streets. Six months later, my brother, by chance, saw me begging on the pavement. He was very sad. But I could not ruin his life. I left for Delhi. My brother later married, but he took to drink. He died in 1990, leaving three children.'

Gurappa begged in Delhi. The railway station was an unofficial shelter for leprosy victims. During the Emergency of 1975, they were evicted. It was then that he came to Faridabad and, with some friends, started a society for self-help of leprosy patients. HelpAge India sponsors 72 individuals over the age of 60.

This initiative has a particular resonance in a country where the family is the sole source of social security: for the old to be alone is another form of mutilation, and leprosy sufferers have had enough of that. The ashram has created another version of extended family, a network of surrogate kin.

There have been many marriages here. Gurappa calls Hossein and Basamma, an elderly Muslim and his Hindu wife. They have two children, and recently a grandchild was born. Then Lamibhai and Mallappa come forward, a tall elderly Dalit and his diminutive *Pandit* wife.

It is a powerful comment on Indian society that this should be a place of complete communal and social harmony. It is a practical embodiment of a religion of humanity, where differences of religion, caste and status are seen for the superficial and arbitrary divisions they are. Does it really require a reductive and excluding sickness for human beings to recognise the common humanity and shared destiny that belong to all of us?

This quiet, unobtrusive spot ought to be not simply the site of uncelebrated survival, for it is a living example of what is possible once we recognise the shared predicament, the leprosy that is, as it were, our existence. It should be a place of pilgrimage, required visiting for politicians and all who sit in high places, that they, too, might learn to live by the same steady light that guides these lives of suffering and solidarity. Here, ageing is not a fate to be dreaded, but a secure journey for people borne up by the tenderness and commitment of others. This serves as a metaphor for the lives of older people: against the discrimination, indifference and hostility of the world, the great majority manage to lead lives of stoic dignity and endurance.

Conclusion

The rising dependency of the retired on the working population has been recognised by many Western governments which have sought to raise the retirement age. In France in May and June 2003, there were widespread strikes against proposals to lengthen the working life. In Austria, too, people took to the streets. In Germany the government is cutting its allowance to the retired, as well as to other beneficiaries of its generous state support.

Does this demonstrate the limits of the 'European' economic model, with its ample welfare provision, as opposed to the US and UK experiences, which expect individuals to make provision for their own old age, with the state providing only a residual security against the most extreme dereliction?

When people demonstrate against the necessity for a longer working life, is this a protest against demographic change? If so, how will this be affected by exhibitions of public anger? How can governments indemnify people against choices, presumably freely made by them, not to have children? Under the threat of racist violence, how can governments open their countries to 'new blood', when it flows through the veins of people whose skin colour is unacceptable to a substantial proportion of the population? What 'policies' can be introduced to combat the decline in fertility? How enduring is this change? Is it not possible that it might all change once more with a shift in economic fortunes?

The phenomenal rise in Japan's economic power was halted in 1989, and this coincided with a decline in the fertility rate to 1.38. With rising life expectancy and controls on immigration, Japan is faced with the most dramatic increase in the proportion of the elderly and a serious funding crisis of its pension commitments. Its efforts to stimulate the economy have resulted in a national debt of almost US $5 trillion, which is 135 per cent of annual output.

Does a declining birth rate reflect economic insecurity, or is it a measure of past economic success? Have the people in the rich world become unwilling to renew their populations because individuals are too concerned with their own self-expression and fulfilment? Or do they fear that the world into which children are to be born offers too little security? Are people inhibited by their anxiety about the kind of world children will inherit? Does our own complicity in the abuse of resources, the poisoning of the elements of life, the violence implicit in an accelerating tempo of consumption, set up feelings of guilt about the kind of life future generations can expect? It is clear that abstention from producing children has little to do with fears for their individual survival – medical science constantly advertises a utopian future which will prolong life further and offer us control over even genetically determined illness. Perhaps this also creates collective doubts over the constantly hyped miracles of technology, which are supposed to bring us a world of perpetual plenty, an absence of pain, a form of transcendence of our own poor human limitations.

Is the concern over an ageing population simply a transient response to the stalling of the global economy in the wake of September 11 and the collapse of share prices? There was, after all, a fear in Britain during the great Depression of the 1930s over a falling population. Will the present extrapolations from a troubled moment also pass away as economic growth resumes and people gain confidence in the future? Will this then encourage them to increase the number of children they have?

In the South, more and more people are surviving into extreme old age. The success of policies of limiting population could scarcely have been achieved if the likelihood of the survival of children into adulthood – and into old age – were not assured. The proportion of elderly people will also increase in India, China, Central and South America and some parts of Africa. Many of these older people will live to see a decline in traditional networks of support by kinsfolk and neighbours. The wealth created in the South is heavily concentrated in the hands of a small minority who have little incentive to replace these decaying mechanisms by structures of welfare which have cushioned a majority of the present generation of the elderly in the rich world against poverty and hardship. Indeed, when they observe efforts by the West to take apart some of these structures and to throw future generations upon their own resources, their reluctance to set up schemes of comprehensive welfare only confirms their prudence in failing to do so.

Or shall we see convergence between the weakening of systems of welfare in the West and the strengthening of some state provision in the South? Will a balance be achieved with modest provision for the least able and most vulnerable in global society, and an expectation that the competent and capable will provide their own protection against old age and abandonment? It is impossible to say. We know that even in Britain there are around 5 million people caring for those weaker or more infirm they are, many them themselves elderly. Perhaps the supports of love and kinship do not decay as readily as we have been led to believe.

There is, perhaps, only a limited ability to predict the future by projecting into it present trends and possibilities. What is certain is that to grow old in insecurity and poverty, which is the fate of the great majority of the elderly in the world, is neither inevitable nor necessary. R. H. Tawney suggested that a civilisation should be judged by the way in which it treats its children. This insight is perhaps even more appropriate today in relation to attitudes towards the elderly. What we see among the elderly is a reflection of the inequalities that affect all other social groups: great differences in the level of economic, social and emotional security, a few of which are a result of individual or idiosyncratic failings, but the majority of which are a consequence of the growing gulf between rich and poor. Old people reflect the great distributive injustices of the world; only for them, these appear in a magnified and aggravated form, since they have for the most part endured lives of labour, privation and insufficiency. As their powers fail they find no certainty of being tended and cared for. What their growing number gives them in terms of potential electoral power is little compared to their waning social power and function all over the world.

This represents yet another wasted resource in a global system which seems to have enshrined dispensability – of resources, of labour, of experience, of wisdom, of memory – at the heart of its restless project of wealth creation. Whether the collective experience, abilities, knowledge and resourcefulness of the elderly can be used for the betterment of the world is unclear. Despite exhortations and ritual humanitarian gestures towards older people, there is as yet little evidence that these qualities are anywhere being taken seriously.

Notes

INTRODUCTION

1. *The History of Thai Laws*, Chanvit Kasetsiri and Vikul Pongpanitanondha (eds), Bangkok, n.d.
2. *Guardian*, August 20, 2002.
3. *Guardian*, August 16, 2002.
4. Wilson, Gail, *Education and Ageing*, Vol. 16, no. 2, 2001.
5. Canada survey, p. 150.
6. Interview with the BBC, April 24, 2002.
7. K.-T. Khaw, 'Globalisation and Support in Old Age', *British Medical Journal*, 1999, cited by Dr Gail Wilson, *Education and Ageing*, Vol. 16, no. 2, 2001.

CHAPTER 1

1. de Beauvoir, Simone, *Old Age*, Penguin, London, 1973.
2. Ibid.
3. Canada Study, *People and Perspectives*, p. 144.
4. Seabrook, Jeremy, *Colonies of the Heart*, GMP, London, 1999.
5. Canada study, p. 144.
6. de Beauvoir, *Old Age*.
7. Ibid.
8. Canada study, p. 144.
9. de Beauvoir, *Old Age*.
10. Malinowski, B., *Magic, Science and Religion*, New York, 1954.
11. Norberg-Hodge, Helena, *Ancient Futures*, Zed Books, London, 1995.
12. Benedict, Ruth, *Patterns of Culture*, Mentor Books, New York, 1946.
13. International Labour Office, *World Labour Report*, Geneva, 2000.
14. Technical Meeting on Population and Aging of the UN Population Fund, 1998.

CHAPTER 2

1. International Longevity Center, *Productive Lives*, http://www.ilcusa.org/pubs/product/pdf

CHAPTER 3

1. WIDO report 1998; website: http://www.oneworld.org.empowering widows/10 countries/Nigeria.html
2. *Straits Times*, Singapore, September 2000.
3. HelpAge Tanzania, personal communication, 2002.

4. Seabrook, Jeremy, *Working Class Childhood*, Victor Gollancz, London, 1982.
5. Fukuyama, Francis, *The End of History and the Last Man*, HarperCollins, New York, 1992.
6. de Beauvoir, Simone, *Old Age*, 1970.
7. *Observer*, January 12, 2002.
8. de Beauvoir, *Old Age*.
9. Ibid.
10. *Journal of Gerontological Social Work*, Vol. 24, 1 and 2, 1995.
11. Johnson, Paul, *Old Age and Ageing in Britain*, ReFRESH, sponsored by the Economic History Society, Autumn 1993.
12. *Guardian*, August 3, 2002.
13. *Policy Review*, June and July 1999.
14. HelpAge International, report 2001.
15. Ibid.
16. Institute of Development Studies, quoted by IRIN, United Nations Humanitarian Information Unit, 2002.

CHAPTER 4

1. Benbo, Zhang, researcher, State Planning Commission, 2001.
2. Bay Fang, 'The Parent-sitters Club', US News and World report, September 4, 2000.
3. HelpAge International, *The Situation of Older People in Vietnam 2000*, London, 2000.

CHAPTER 5

1. OECD, Policy Brief, December 2001.
2. HelpAge International, *The State of the World's Older People*, London, 2002.
3. Woolf, Linda M., Webster University, St Louis, Missouri, 1998.
4. *National Elder Abuse Incidence Study*, Final Report, National Aging Information Center, Washington, 1998.

Useful Contacts

HelpAge International
P.O. Box 32832
London
N1 9ZN
Email: hai@helpage.org
www.helpage.org

HelpAge India
C-14, Qutab Institutional Area
New Delhi 110-016
India
www.helpageindia.com

HelpAge publishes research, statistics and the testimonies of older people from all over the world. It is a global network of not-for-profit organisations, and works specifically with disadvantaged older people everywhere.

Help the Aged
207–221 Pentonville Road
London
N1 9UZ
Email: info@helptheaged.org.uk
www.helptheaged.org.uk

Help the Aged is committed to addressing the issues that matter to older people. They have four main priorities: combating poverty, reducing Isolation, defeating ageism and challenging poor care standards. Working together with older people they campaign, research and develop practical solutions.

Age Concern
1268 London Road
London
SW16 4ER
www.ageconcern.org.uk
Information Line (in UK only): 0800 009966

Age Concern is an UK network of more than 400 independent charities, second only to the British government in providing high-quality help and care for older people in the UK. Age Concern supports all people over 50 in the UK, ensuring that they get the most from life. They provide essential services such as day care and information and campaign on issues such as age discrimination and pensions, and work to influence public opinion and government policy about older people.

Seniors Network
www.seniorsnetwork.co.uk

Seniors Network is an information resource for older people and their organisations. It is completely independent and is not allied to any other type of organisation.

National Institute on Aging
Building 31, Room 5C27
31 Center Drive, MSC 2292
Bethesda
MD 20892
USA
www.nia.nih.gov

National Institute on Aging is one of the 25 institutes and centres of the National Institutes of Health. It leads a broad scientific effort to understand the nature of ageing and to extend the healthy, active years of life.

International Longevity Center – USA
60 East 86th Street,
New York
NY 10028
USA
www.ilcusa.org
Email: info@ilcusa.org

International Longevity Center is a not-for-profit, nonpartisan research, policy and education organisation, set up to help societies address the issues of population ageing and longevity in positive and constructive ways, and to highlight older people's productivity and contributions to their families and to society as a whole. It is an independent affiliate of Mount Sinai School of Medicine.

Canadian Association of Retired Persons
Fifty-Plus.net
Suite 300
27 Queen Street East
Toronto, Ontario
M5C 2M6
Canada
www.50plus.com

The leading Canadian website providing unique content, community and commerce for people over the age of 50. The online home of CARP, Canada's largest 50+ advocacy group, with more than 400,000 members, and for *CARPNews 50Plus* magazine, Canada's largest 50+ publication.

Canadian Center for Activity and Aging
1490 Richmond Street
London,
Ontario N6G 2M3
Canada
www.uwo.ca/actage/
Advocacy Group ccaa@uwo.ca

The Center's mission is to develop, encourage and promote an active, healthy lifestyle for Canadian adults that will enhance the dignity of the ageing process.

Seniors Policies and Programs Database (SPPD)
www.sppd.gc.ca

The SPPD is a database of Canadian government policies and programmes for which seniors are the primary beneficiaries.